GANG

FIT

Freedom & Strength

www.guruanaerobic.com

ISBN 979-8-415377-18-3

CONTENTS

PART ONE

PART TWO

PART THREE

- PART ONE -

Much of Gang Fit's content contradicts the usual advice – if you follow it you will inevitably get grief from many sections of society. This is what happens when you start thinking for yourself. The majority of adults are modern-day slaves, do as they say and you'll end up the same way. From the very first page they will hate this book - they'll say its message is anti-social and encourages bad behavior. Yes, bad behavior *as they see it*. If you want to be an individual when you're older, and not a clone, you will *have to be different to them*. This means breaking rules.

Oldies have become fossilised, stuck in their ways, unable to see things the way you do. Furthermore, their physical condition has deteriorated to the point where the fuckers can hardly run for a bus. They have no pride. This book is only 'anti-social' in their world, not yours. What you're doing is building a strong physique, an independent mind, and a warrior spirit. That's something to be proud of.

You are young, you have dreams and ambitions. Inside you there is something wild, powerful, and unstoppable - something waiting to be unleashed. Adults had this once; now they haven't. This is what they're scared of, so they call it bad behaviour. So, be prepared for a fight, because that's what you're going to get.

You Decide

People are constantly telling you what you should do, how to behave and how to live your life - but before you follow the herd, look at the individuals who are telling you this. What do they look like? Do you want to be like them? Gang Fit shows you a different way. Aren't you sick and tired of listening to the constant jabber about education, university, and employment? Adults say that all that shit is the reality of life - "Billy! Money doesn't grow on trees you know, be responsible, you've got to pass your exams and get a job!" Listen very carefully - that is their reality, it doesn't have to be yours. If you do it, you *will* get somewhere in life but it *won't* be the place you want it to be. This is the point; it does work but it doesn't work for you. *It's not what you want.*

In reality there are probably less than five people on the planet who *really* want you to do well in life. No one else gives a shit. Some young people can't seem to deal with this, so they write awful poetry and pretend to self-harm. That's not the answer; fighting is. You need to fight and bust-up the usual way of doing things. Be aware though that being independent and rejecting the rules and conventions that don't suit you will severely wind people up - in an attempt to put you down they'll bracket you as mindless, argumentative, juvenile and aggressive. Fuck them - your life is yours.

At the same time as fighting the brain-dead you also need to declare war on yourself - your own insecurities and weaknesses. This is the real challenge. Your own mind is what holds you back the most. Your weaknesses, fears, and timidity are like ballistic missiles that will destroy your ambitions and kill your attempts at progress. The most important thing for you to do, far more important than exams and degrees, is to assassinate your weak mind and replace it with a warrior mind.

From now on, *decide what you want* and ignore all the crap that others vomit. Shed any low-level attitude you may have about yourself. Build your body and strengthen your mind. Approach things like you're some sort of scientist - experiment on yourself, test your limits and push the boundaries. Unleash the wild beast inside you and live free or die trying.

Smash Up the World

Some fool once told me, "the world doesn't owe you a living", but the crusty old coffin-dodger didn't have the brains to comprehend the flipside, that the free individual doesn't owe the world either. You don't owe anything to anybody, especially those individuals who think they have some sort of authority over you. Oh, I forgot…the world doesn't have to do shit for you but *you have to do what you're told*? What sort of arrangement is that? Were you asked about this?

10

Every person on the planet was born out of a woman's vagina, just like you. They were naked and covered with blood and crap, just like you. They had their umbilical cord cut, just like you. For a whole year they pissed and shitted themselves, just like you. No one has authority over you.

Smash up the world.

Smash up the people who tell you what to do. Smash up the person who tries to intimidate you. Smash them up. Smash up their ideals. Smash up their beliefs. Smash up their authority. You have to stir up trouble if you want to achieve anything or be your own person. In reality, when you think, talk, and act like a free individual, trouble will come your way whether you want it or not because it's in the nature of slaves to despise the free.

Young people like you are constantly being blamed for the ills of society; how can this be? You didn't make this society, adults did; if there are any problems they are to blame. So, you might as well ignore them and their concerns. The World is yours now whether they like it or not.

****

Your mental attitude is the most important possession you will ever own – more important than the strength of your biceps, the size of your winky or how much money you have in your bank account. A weak, fearful and timid attitude means you'll be at the mercy of any tom, dick or harry(iet). Your attitude determines whether you'll be a victim or a success.

The child is born a genius but by the time it gets to middle-age it has become a complete idiot. Since you were born, adults and teachers have been filling your head with their ideas – what to think, what to like, and how to live. The problem is this - if you follow advice from a slave you'll become a slave. Unless you're some sort of retard you wouldn't deliberately choose to become a slave, but it happens in slow motion without you noticing. The whole system is set up so that you'll believe there is no other way – and slowly, slowly, you'll start to believe the system is actually good for you. Your brainwashing is then complete.

When you allow people to control and determine your life, you just become a performing flea. Go to your nearest railway station at rush hour; you'll see the performing fleas going to work - every morning going through the same routine; collecting in their little groups on the same spot of the same platform, waiting for the train to deliver them to their jobs – a sort of living hell.

11

And they tell you slavery is history?

One of the most exhilarating opening five minutes of any film is from '*28 Weeks Later*'. The main character, Don, is running for his life from flesh-eating zombies that have broken into the house where he is hiding out. The zombies kill all the occupants, but he manages to escape by jumping into the front garden from an upstairs bedroom window. He pelts across a field – the zombies are new-skool fuckers in that they're fast like track sprinters. Luckily, just before Don is about to get his brains eaten, he comes across a speedboat moored on a nearby river and manages to get away; the boat's propeller mashing up a few Z's in the process.

The thing about zombies is that they don't just kill you – you die, then you become one of them. In the same way, adults say they're educating you and showing you how to get on in life – but they're not, they're just trying to turn you into mini-versions of themselves. Just like the zombies, they are doing their best to destroy your brain and obliterate your identity.

Discover Different Worlds Without a Spaceship

TASK - Rather than sleep, stay up all night. Don't go to bed. At 1am leave your house and wander the streets. Do this with mates or on your own, and wear something dark so you'll blend into the background. Things you never notice during the day will show themselves; new sights, new sounds, different people, perhaps some weird shit. Observe the movements and shenanigans of the cat, the fox, the rat, the tramp and the drunk. Take note of the shady characters and individuals who inhabit the nocturnal world. This is the realm of the vampire, the werewolf, and all the other dark entities of horror stories. Whilst these entities only exist in imagination, the night can still be an eerie and dangerous place. Climb over walls, wander downs alleys and investigate empty buildings - you'll discover places previously unknown to you.

If you're in the city, go to the 'red-light' district and check out what's going on. Stay out 'til dawn and see how things change - cars start intruding on the night, council sweepers start appearing, the birds start singing, and the zombie nation begins its commute to work.

You won't find this in your school's curriculum, yet it's outside your front door, one-third of the day you don't really know about. They tell you to get a good night's sleep so you'll be fresh for class; do the opposite – sleep at school and investigate the night.

Note: It may be that you'll be stopped by the cops in a patrol car, "Wot you up to lads? Why are you out at this time? Shouldn't you be in bed? Where you going? Where d'you live? Wot's in your pockets?" Just say you're going for a stroll - there's no law against that is there?

As soon as you start doing your own thing, even like going for a walk at night, you get hassled. All 'normal' people should be tucked up in bed.

There are many different worlds. Your upbringing conditions you to exist in only one - the 9 to 5 world of work and all the usual shit. Your parents don't show you there are other ways of living, neither do your teachers – it's almost as if they're keeping you ignorant on purpose.

Here's what to do: Stop whatever you're doing for one week and start to investigate other worlds. Do things you don't normally do and visit places you don't normally visit. Speak to people you wouldn't normally speak to. You'll notice that the lives of some people are completely different to yours and far different to the mainstream.

Don't Leave Your Education to School

Most teachers are teaching you garbage – don't listen to them. Many of the things they say are important are *not* important and many things they say are not important or don't even talk about, *are* important - some very important. Look at the successful people you know, what are they expert at?

People say that school prepares you for life in the big, wide world – it does nothing of the sort. Your teachers tell you this, but look at them, they have no money; they can barely afford the rent for their crap accommodation. How are they able to advise you about being successful in life? In a way they can't be blamed, they just don't know any different. Even though the world has endless possibilities and opportunities, they have been conditioned by their background to believe their way is the best way – ignore them; leave them to their version of the world.

Teachers and other goons will come up with examples of individuals who have done well by education; passed exams, went to university, got good jobs and so on - what they don't speak about are the untold thousands who haven't benefited from this in any way. And they'll ignore the people you look up to who have done it by completely different means. This is not saying that knowledge is not necessary, of course it is, but there is classroom knowledge and *real world* knowledge, the sort that will help you in your life. Furthermore, school is mostly teaching you to rely on someone else to feed you, clothe you, and house you. It's telling you that you have to become "more employable" by learning lots of unnecessary facts and useless shit.

Your school also tells you that you need to work hard to achieve success; well, take a walk down any high street and you'll see many hard-working people collecting rubbish, delivering the post, driving buses, working in shops and sweeping the streets (there's nothing wrong with that if that's what you want, but if you've got half a brain it shouldn't be what you want). Then there are the jokers who work in offices, living the same routine everyday – hardly better than brain-dead zombies. The idea that you'll get somewhere *just* by "working hard" is the biggest lie of all. Many millions of people work very hard yet have got nowhere in life. You can see the evidence of that all around you

The problem with school is that it forces kids to learn stuff they hate or are no good at; for some reason this is backed up by most parents.

There is absolutely no reason to do stuff that you don't like doing. Decide what is important at school and do that. If you love history immerse yourself in it. If you hate geography do the bare minimum, or better still, drop it completely. From now on, do what you're interested in – not what others say you should be interested in. Some teachers and educators will say there's no need to learn Latin as it's not needed in today's world. Well, if it's interesting to you, learn it. That's good enough. So, this is not saying that you shouldn't do anything as that won't get you anywhere – just follow what you want and ignore anything else.
We are constantly being told that knowledge is power and that education is the passport to a better career, more opportunity, and so on – if you live in a poor African village that's true but here it's not. In modern societies, the belief that more education, more information and more knowledge guarantee a *better life* is completely untrue.
If you are having difficulty at school, don't worry – the real education is outside school. Furthermore, if you hate school there's nothing wrong with you, it's a perfectly natural reaction to being caged.

Being locked inside the same building five days a week, doing what you're told with losers your own age, is good for you? People who believe that will believe anything.

Dynamic Endurance

TASK – find a half-mile (800m) route in your neighbourhood – don't have any warm up, just go outside and start running; fast as you can…don't stop, keep going. When your breathing gets difficult or your legs start feeling heavy, back off for a few seconds then speed up again. When you've finished wait five minutes then repeat. Do this twice a week for 6 weeks - by then you'll virtually be able to sprint all the way.

In the US they have a horse called a Quarter Horse, it's bred specifically to sprint distances from 100m to 800m - some have been clocked at 55mph (88 km/h) which isn't much slower than a cheetah. They can cover 400m in 20seconds and 800m in less than a minute. If you train like a Quarter Horse you will develop the sort of fitness that you need to run from the Law - the majority of coppers have eaten far too many doughnuts to be able to keep up with that.

If you want you can extend the distance to ¾ or even 1 mile – but no further! You want a strong, athletic, and dynamic body – not the fragile

'fitness' of a marathon runner. Long distance running will make you weedy and skinny, and in the process, kill any natural speed you have. Endurance should *always* be built in at a fast or dynamic pace.

Note: Why no warm-up? Well, in what real-life situation would you be able to do a warm-up? You may be running for your life. There's a gang wanting to give you a beating or the fuzz are chasing you – "Oh, excuse me, would you mind giving me a few minutes to do a warm-up?"

It's said that a horse can be pushed until it runs itself to death; don't know how it dies, perhaps its heart explodes, You can run a ½ mile so fast that you'll think your chest is going to burst – don't worry, it won't. What *will* happen is that your physiology will undergo such a remarkable transformation that you'll turn into the human equivalent of a Quarter Horse.

Some other sessions to try (on track, road or grass):

1/ Sprint 200m (or 30secs) as fast as you can - rest for three minutes and repeat. Session is finished when you have completed six runs.

2/ Run 400m (or 70secs) non-stop - rest for five minutes. Repeat three times.

3/ Run 300m fast (or 45secs) - rest for 90 seconds then sprint 150m (around 20secs). Rest for five minutes. Repeat twice.

4/ Find a reasonably steep hill. Run up for 150m. Slowly walk down. The session is over when you've completed six runs.

Note: This type of training is called 'Interval Training' - where you run a certain distance, rest and repeat. There are many variations you can try, the distances can be anywhere from 60 to 1000m with recoveries (rest) from 30secs to 10mins, or more.

TASK – You may have heard of high knees, basically 'running on the spot'. The target here is to do 300 in one go. This is pretty tough; after a while your upper legs will begin to feel heavy, but keep going and make sure you are bringing your thighs up parallel to the ground. Your posture should be upright throughout, not leaning back, and keep on the balls of your feet. If you can't do the full amount straight away split it into two sets (with a minute or two between each set). As you progress, you'll be able to do more in the first set until you can complete the whole 300. Once you've achieved this try using some two-kilogram ankle weights, they don't cost much, and work up to 300 reps again. Do this twice a week together with your interval training.

Additional task: Every two months complete one thousand high knees – then take a week off from *all* exercise. The stimulus to your system will force your body to adapt to a higher level. You can split up the full amount into any number of sets as long as you complete the total.

High knees and interval training are very demanding and severely tax the lower limbs; furthermore, the heart, lungs, and circulatory system are challenged well beyond the regular demands of long distance or aerobic training. The burn you feel in your muscles during this type of exercise is caused by the buildup of lactic acid (specifically, hydrogen ions) - known as 'acidosis'. Lactic acid is produced because the energetic demands of the exercise can't be totally covered by the amount of oxygen you breathe in, so some of the energy has to be produced anaerobically (without oxygen) – lactic acid is the by-product of this anaerobic process. The ability to tolerate acidosis, physiologically and psychologically, is the first thing older people lose. Make it your friend.

The Educated Idiot

In many ways the more education you get the more of an idiot you become. Here's an example: A person flips a coin ninety-nine times in a row, each time it's a head; what is the probability that the hundredth flip will be a tail? Someone clueless in maths would most likely say zero or "hardly any chance". Conversely, someone who is good at maths would answer 50/50, i.e., there's an equal likelihood of heads or tails. At school that answer would be right, as each flip of the coin is unaffected by previous flips; in the real world however, that answer would make you a sucker. The right answer is zero. The 'clueless' person was right. Think about it; the likelihood of someone throwing ninety-nine heads in a row is a zillion to one – you are being conned. The coin is loaded. Ask an adult, they usually get this wrong – ask a ten or eleven-year old, they'll get it right. Most kids on the street will realise straight away they are being conned.

You are not taught to think at school, that is not the aim of academic education. You are spoon-fed information so you can pass exams in subjects educationists have decided are for your benefit. They decide the subjects and they decide the questions. All education is doing is telling you what you need to know so you can answer the questions they've set. If you program a robot to make a cup of tea, it won't be able to bake a cake. If you are programmed in a certain way at school, you lose the ability to think in other ways.

Here is another question that you might have difficulty answering, even though it's straightforward if you have a clear head. There are two cups, one filled with black tea (no milk), the other just milk. Take a teaspoon of milk from the second cup and stir it into the black tea. Now take a teaspoon of liquid from that cup and stir it into the cup with the milk.

Q: Is there more milk in the black tea cup than tea in the milk cup?

The more maths you've been taught at school the less chance you'll be able to answer. This is because your school teaches you maths in a way which makes you unable to understand numbers. They've messed up your mind.

This is how people become educated idiots – they learn 'facts', statistics, dates, geography, history, biology, etc. Unknown to them, most of the facts are untrue, only partly true, or completely irrelevant. However, the more exams they pass and the more certificates they get, the more they believe they know what they're talking about. If *you* want to become an educated idiot believe everything you learn at school or university.

The next time someone boasts how intelligent they are because they've passed loads of exams – feel sorry for the idiot…or knock their head off. That will be a new lesson for them.

Become Unemployable

If you tell most adults you don't want a job, they will react like you said their baby has a face like a camel's arse. Try it out and see for yourself. It's pretty funny how predictable and brainwashed people are. These morons are shallower than a puddle of cat's piss; they're outraged because "you're a lazy, good-for-nothing waste of space with a bad attitude". Apparently, it's your duty to "contribute to society" #suckmydick

Shit-for-brains will tell you that wearing a paper hat and working for Tesco is better than nothing. Shit-for-brains cousin will tell you, "there's pride in work". Shit-for-brains mum will say, "what makes you think you're so special?" Advice: shift-delete these idiots from your life - being surrounded by 'shit-for-brains' will turn *your* brains to shit.

You do eleven years at school so you can wear a paper hat? Fuck that. Most jobs you'll be wearing a 'paper hat' of some sort - a tie, a suit, a uniform or some other crap which shows that someone owns you. You see those poor suckers in supermarkets? Forced to wear flashing reindeer antlers at Christmas - where's the pride in that?

People who base their self-pride on being employed are the sort of idiots who die six months after they've retired; their minds are so undeveloped they have nothing to live for.

If you're ever in the unfortunate position of having a job make sure it's only temporary; if you carry on with it you'll be trapped like a fly in a spider's web. It is far more satisfying refusing a job than accepting one. Always work on your own project or idea – music, training, acting, dancing, business, crime, travel, sport, writing, rearing goats or building a space rocket.
If you're in a job now, think seriously about what you're doing – you'll likely find that it's pointless. If you do pointless things you'll become a pointless person.

Being 'unemployable' means that you're allergic to taking orders, as any real man should be. Develop self-reliance and decide your own direction in life. Once you've tasted freedom the world of work feels like slavery.

Survive Without Money

This is a disconcerting test. Disconcerting because it holds a mirror up to your own bullshit about how honest you think you are.

Survive without money for two weeks. That doesn't sound like much does it? But I mean have nothing except your accommodation. Where do you get food from? Perhaps you'll decide not to eat for two weeks – not likely. Would you steal food? Would you shoplift? Would you eat other peoples' leftovers? Perhaps you would scavenge from supermarket skips or thrown away food from street markets?

When the shit gets tough you may be surprised at what you would do to survive. You may convince yourself it's only a temporary situation, so you have to break some rules to get you through…but there's no such thing as a temporary crime is there?
When you know your dark side, the things you would do or consider doing when the going gets seriously tough, you become less concerned about other peoples' deficits.

All notions of civilization fall away when survival is at stake. Don't listen to comfortable people who say, "I would never do that" – they are bullshitters. Circumstances make people do all sorts of unholy things. Try and avoid being in a situation where you have to do something awful to survive - work on something better. But when things are hard, you have to do what you can to get through. That's the harsh reality. Accept it and understand you're not perfect, no one is.

Don't be hard on yourself for not being perfect, but you should be hard on yourself for being a weak, whiney, pathetic victim – the universe hates weaklings, evolution gets rid of them.

Somatotype

Somatotype refers to the build or physical structure of a person (*soma* = Greek for *body*). There are three main classifications: Ectomorph, Mesomorph and Endomorph.

Ectomorph: Long and thin muscles/limbs; appearance is slim or skinny. Ectomorphs find it hard to put on muscle and are resistant to putting on fat. They make good endurance athletes, rock-climbers, high jumpers, and light-weight boxers or martial artists. The incomparable Bruce Lee was an ectomorph – if you've never heard of Bruce Lee, where you at?

Mesomorph: Characterised by an athletic and muscular physique. Mesomorphs build muscle easily. They make good all-round athletes, being fast, strong and lean.

Endomorph: The biggest of the three somatotypes. The endomorph has a heavy bone structure and a predisposition to accumulate fat. However, underneath the fat is usually plenty of muscle. Well trained endomorphs make good weight-lifters, shot-putters and all types of strength athletes.

	Ectomorph	Mesomorph	Endomorph
Bone Structure	Light	Medium	Heavy
Physique	Thin	Athletic	Thick-set
Absolute Strength	Poor	very good	very good
Relative Strength	Good	very good	Poor
Endurance	very good	Good	Poor
Agility	very good	very good	Poor
Top Speed	Good	very good	Poor

Many people are a mix of two or even all three types.

It may look like the mesomorph has the main advantages but whether something is an advantage is context dependent.

Ecto – Agile and quick; can run rings round an opponent making them look foolish and lumbering. Can run and run. Has the sting of a mosquito; cannot be caught.

Meso – Athletic and gymnastic; resilient and durable. All-rounders.

Endo – The strongest of the lot; has the potential to develop crushing strength. The destructive power of a tank.

There's a saying that you can't turn a carthorse into a race horse; whilst this is mostly true, it is possible to make the carthorse *faster*. The ectomorph can train to run faster than most mesomorphs, and the endomorph can make themselves as lean as any ectomorph. So don't worry if you're "naturally" this or that. Further, in the real world there are many scenarios, options, challenges, and opportunities - be aware of your natural limitations or advantages, but life is too multifaceted to argue that your traits alone determine your success in life.

Mental Strength and Fearlessness

There are many physically strong individuals who are psychologically weak. You may know some. Their minds are fragile. They cry and moan because their girlfriend left them or their pet chinchilla got accidently flushed down the toilet. More importantly, they are unreliable in a crisis, disappearing when the going gets tough – these people are worse than your biggest enemy; they will always let you down, undermining your plans and efforts. They are a form of cancer – get rid of them.

Physical strength without psychological strength is virtually useless, like an elephant being scared of a mouse.

If you are mentally weak and afraid, no matter what 'weapons' you may have you will be firing blanks – your strengths will fall short at critical times. If you're scared of physical or psychological pain you will never, ever, overcome your weaknesses.
You know what you're scared of. You know when you run from danger. The danger can be real or in your head; talking in front of a group or facing up to someone bigger than you.

The woodcutter knows that the strongest tree comes from the edge of the wood that has been battered by the wind. This is the same for you. To become tough you have to open yourself up to frightening situations so that over time your fears decrease, until eventually they become nothing. If you can't find any frightening or challenging situations *you and your friends should go out of your way to create some.*

20

The Japanese Samurai warriors had a way of dealing with fear…

In *'Hagakure: The book of the Samurai'*, by Yamamoto Tsunetomo - The Master advises the student Samurai thus, "Meditation on inevitable death should be performed daily when one's body and mind are at peace, one should meditate upon being ripped apart by arrows, rifles, spears and swords, being carried away by surging waves, being thrown into the midst of a great fire, being struck by lightning, being shaken to death by a great earthquake, falling from thousand-foot cliffs, dying of disease or committing seppuku at the death of one's master. And every day without fail one should consider himself dead".

Note: 'Seppuku' is ritual suicide by cutting your stomach open.

The Samurai master is saying to his students that the way to become fearless is to think yourself dead already – once you're no longer fear death or physical harm, you are scared of no one. The only way that someone can dominate you is if you are in fear of them or the consequences of what they can do. If you are 'already dead' in your mind you become impervious to threats or potentially frightening situations.
Once you've forged your body and mind to cope with the demands of the Street, when someone tries to push you around you will be prepared - they will regret it.

Warning: You should be pragmatic and not suicidally heroic…there are some situations that even a Gorilla would have to escape from. When you're outnumbered you may have to run, climb, jump or disappear into the background…"now you see me, now you don't". Use your brain - there is no shame in running or backing down when the odds are against you. That isn't fear, that's commonsense.

CHALLENGE - Go with a friend or group of friends to your local high street on a shopping day. Whilst everyone is walking around this way and that, your aim is to walk in an absolute straight line down the middle of the pavement for at least 100metres. Your mates have to watch to make sure you don't deviate. After you've done this, it is their turn. This is a surprisingly tough challenge - you will come under intense pressure to get out of the way of some people. People will mutter under their breath, some might call you names, some may even threaten you – no matter, keep your resolve. Most people will fail this test first time and some will always fail. If you mess up the first time have another go until you have the psychological fortitude to complete it properly. If you're fearless you'll be able to do it. You may need your friends if any trouble flares up.

Bonus – this is hilarious to watch.

Fearlessness and mental strength are more important than confidence. You can't be confident at everything, that's impossible, but you can have the guts to try. In any endeavour there comes a point when your confidence may desert you, don't worry about this, it shows you have reached the edge of your comfort zone – this is the territory that *every* successful individual or warrior inhabits. There is no exception to this. Whatever path you decide to follow, if you take it seriously you will repeatedly hit the outer boundaries of what you can cope with. This is where your true toughness is tested. No book can give you this – you have to face it for yourself in the real world.

Obliteration

Mass control requires the obliteration of your identity. Whether it's society, religion or some other nonsense, either they control you by force (which creates resistance) or more effectively, they control you by your consent. As soon as you don't consent you become an apostate, and apostates are hated by everyone including the people who are still zombies.

Try this test: Live with people who work nine to five. Wake up after they've left for work. Be in before they get home from work. Go out to parties during the week. Get up early on a Sunday. Go to the gym on a Tuesday mid-morning. Stay up late during the week. Basically, have a different timetable to them. Even though you may be perfectly nice and pay your way, they will notice you are not like them, not stuck to their schedules. As sure as a bear shits in the woods they will begin to hate you. See for yourself. Slaves detest the free.

There's only one certain thing in life – your death. Death is your complete obliteration. You'll only remain in memory, or maybe if you're very lucky, in some sort of legacy. Eventually even the people who knew or loved you will die - even the *memory* of you will be erased. So, what's the point of being obliterated *before you die*? Your consent and subservience to everything that society expects of you is the obliteration of your independence and personal identity.

As soon as you start school your conditioning and entrapment begins. Then when you leave school your conditioning continues, until you end up like all the other idiots commuting to work. Many working people aren't happy with their lives, many aren't even happy with their long-term relationships – they are trapped.
To escape this you need to become a one-man-army, a force of nature. Smash things up, create havoc, destroy things, destroy the old you, get used to hardship; endure the feast and famine. You will need to become 'insane'. You'll also need to grow a force-field around you to shield you from the people and forces who want to destroy your ambition and individuality.

You'll make loads of mistakes…some of which may have permanent psychological effects - some good, some bad. Ignore the bullshit entrepreneur books about failing, falling, picking yourself up and continuing. When people fail, they usually take people down with them – some may be friends, associates or relatives. This is the hardest part, there are hardly any clean failures, they're messy.

But you have to try, because what awaits you is death and the death of all your loved ones. Your obliteration is certain. But your obliteration before your death is up to you.

Out of Work in Summertime

Being unemployed with your mates in summertime is great - whilst everyone else is cooped up at work you're as free as a bird.

The city in summer is an incredible place to be, full of possibilities.

A fraction of the things you can do:

- Cycle, skate, and discover the city with your mates
- Swim in the rivers/canals/lakes
- Find a wall and paint a mural
- Do circuit training outdoors
- Devise challenges and tests of strength and courage
- Go to as many parties as possible
- Chill out in parks and green spaces.
- Go to the coast in your mate's car (or avoid the ticket inspector on the train)
- If you're that way inclined, in most cities the galleries and museums are free.
- Create videos with your mates and post on the Internet
- Turn your gang into a business
- Find your nearest athletics track and do the Beer-Mile challenge
- Set up some sort of event - music, sport, dance, etc
- Construct a 'boat' out of materials you can find, and float down the river
- Shoot a film
- Cause mayhem

Resist the pressure to find work. The answer to doing nothing is not "getting a job", that is pure slave mentality. It may well be that you have time to kill but no money to spend, so you're going to have to be creative. A tough person isn't crushed by having no money, it motivates them – go out and get it, earn it, make it, print it, win it; anything! Use your imagination.

Make the most of the summer you have. Enjoy yourself. At the same time you should keep your eyes open for money making opportunities…they're all around.

[Beer-Mile Challenge: On a standard 400m athletics track - at the start line, drink a pint of beer then run one lap; on completion of the first lap drink another pint of beer and then run a second lap. Do this until you have completed four laps and drunk four pints of beer. Cans of beer, lager or cider can be used instead of pints. Time how long it takes to complete and compare with your friends]

Brotherhood

There may be times when you and your brothers have your backs against the wall. You are overrun with no escape; in which case you will have to fight like demons. Your inevitable war wounds will be badges of honour, and your scars the sign of a fighter. Over time you'll get to know whom you can rely upon when trouble comes calling. They'll have earned their stripes and your trust - they are your army.

The Mafia have a Code of Honour called *Omertà* which implies that its members must never, ever, cooperate with the police, even when one of them has been a victim of a crime. A person should avoid interfering in the business of others, and absolutely must not inform the authorities of a crime under any circumstances - though if justified he may personally avenge an attack on himself or on his family by Vendetta. Even if somebody is convicted of a crime he has not committed, he is supposed to serve the sentence without giving the police any information about the real criminal, even if that criminal has nothing to do with the Mafia. It is deeply demeaning and shameful to betray even one's deadliest enemy to the police. Within Mafia culture, breaking Omertà is punishable by death.

The State and the police say you shouldn't sort things out for yourself, but the real street warrior doesn't listen to that shit – sort out your own problems. Be good to people who support you, ignore people who have nothing to do with you and deal with people who are working against you.
You must do anything for your brothers; if one is in need, no matter what you're doing and no matter what time of day, you must drop everything to help him. He would do the same for you. A gang, business or enterprise cannot survive without loyalty and solidarity.

One way society tries to control you is to separate you from your friends and undermine your support; but the strength of ten loyal brothers who would die for each other is magnified ten times. Like the Hydra of Greek mythology - when one head is severed two more grow in its place.

24

TASK - Get together with your mates and discuss some sort of project or scheme that you can start - music, sport, art, money…anything. It can be a completely new idea or something you've seen others do. Draw up a plan and decide who does what based on individual strengths and talents. Utilise the resources you can find. Don't worry about small mistakes, they can be ironed out as you go along. Don't tell anyone outside the group what you're doing unless it is helps you in your aims. With the power of five or ten friends you'll be surprised at what you can achieve. Don't stop there. Carry on. You'll find that your life will start to diverge from the masses who go about their lives with their heads in the sand.

In creating something special there'll be challenges you will have to overcome, some seemingly insurmountable; this is when a strong network of loyal and reliable friends comes into its own. *Always* stick by your brotherhood.

Asteroid Threat and You

Draw the curtains, turn off any noise and switch off the lights. Sit very still - don't move. Can you feel it? Can you sense something? The Earth is traveling through space at 20,000mph – that's twenty-six times the speed of sound. Our planet is spinning on its axis as it revolves around the Sun, and our solar system is travelling through the Milky Way which is speeding through the Universe. This has been the case for billions of years. All this is happening without anyone noticing.
Here's the thing: In the grand scheme of space and time you're nothing. In essence, your life is meaningless, so it's up to you to *give it some meaning*. Don't spend your life being a soft, weak, stupid, pathetic coward, afraid to do this, too scared to do that. At any moment an asteroid could collide with Earth – you could be obliterated at any time...the *whole* planet could be smashed to pieces. Will God or any other devine being give a shit about you? Of course not. The same way you don't give a damn about the life of an ant.

TEST – For the next two weeks, if you're always good...be bad; and if you're always bad...be good. Being the opposite of how you normally are is a great way to become mentally strong and open up new experiences and opportunities. All weak people are stuck in the same old habits, unable to break out of behaviours and beliefs which makes them fools. Many older people are experts at being fools in this sense, their brains are fossilised.
Rather than thoughtlessly acting on impulse - curb your instincts and control your actions. This is not saying that the way you are now is wrong, just that you need to be aware of the possible limitations in the way you think and act.

For the goody-two-shoes - the reason you are good isn't that you've been "raised properly" and have morals; it's because you are scared of acting bad. You are fearful of the consequences of acting bad and you don't have the confidence to face confrontation - you are timid. You have thought bad things but you don't have the courage to carry them out. You may convince yourself that logic and reason stop you from doing bad things, but that's just an excuse covering up your fear. Now is the time to stop using your niceness as a mask and do what you feel inside. Be a man.

For the badass - you are scared of being nice through fear of people thinking it's a weakness. So you act tough. Further, you may be paranoid that everyone is down on you on purpose – which can't possibly be true.
If you're bad because you "like being bad" you will ultimately become a victim of your own foolishness and limited thinking. There are times to be bad and there are times to be good – recognize the difference and start to control your destiny. You never get time back, so start now.

Unleash the Beast

Michelangelo di Lodovico Buonarroti Simoni was a 16th century Italian sculptor, painter, architect and poet. Known simply as Michelangelo, many consider him one of the greatest artists to have ever lived. He had something interesting to say about making a sculpture - he said that when he was carving a piece of marble he was only revealing what was already inside, the statue was already there, waiting to be uncovered. *This is the case for you as well.* Inside you there's an atomic force - a force of Nature. It is up to you to let it out before it dies, as it has with many of the older people around you. It's the genie in the bottle. If you harness it for your own benefit you will become virtually unstoppable. You may think this force only exists in atomic bombs and nuclear power stations, when in fact it exists in everything. From the tiniest microorganisms under your feet to giant stars bigger than our entire solar system, everything has this force. All of the people who have utilised its raw energy to the max have become great leaders, great criminals, great minds, great athletes, great warriors – individuals who have shaped the history of the world. This is the 'Beast' waiting to be unleashed.

People are doing their best to stop you from developing it because they are scared of it. Developed to its fullest extent it is fucking fearsome. It doesn't care about good, bad, or any place in-between. Love, co-operation, empathy, caring for the weak and all the things a civilised society goes on about - to atomic force all that is bullshit, it can destroy it in a second. It could (and will eventually) smash up the world without hesitation.

Albert Einstein, the famous theoretical physicist, showed that a single atom has enough energy to set off an unstoppable chain reaction. If you tap into your innate energy you could use it to create something awesome, something special…something which takes you to a level you would have thought unobtainable.

How to start:

Face your fears. Do the things you normally shy away from. *Unleashing the beast* means that your mind has to become like tempered steel - that won't happen if you're timid like a mouse.

Don't be scared of pain. To get stronger and tougher you have to embrace the idea of pain. Get someone to punch you in the face, take your licks. Pain is a good thing in that it tells you to take your hand out of a flame; fear of pain, however, becomes a self-limitation, an excuse not to attempt something. This is what you have to overcome.

Eliminate negative people. If you want to build an empire you need constructive ideas and thoughts - there should be no room for negative and cynical individuals. Negative people love spreading their negativity around. They will discourage your efforts because they are losers, and losers don't like winners. Look carefully at the people around you – if any are negative about you or your potential, drop them immediately from your life.

Build your body. There's a saying that, "you can't fire a cannonball from a canoe". No wild beast is soft and weak, how would it survive in the wild? Modern life weakens your body. If you want to be a warrior, build your body so it becomes like a battleship.

Don't take "no" for an answer. If you need to do something important to advance your cause, don't accept "no". You've been told it's polite to ask, and so it is, but you will never get anywhere if you listen to what people say you can or can't do. Only at school do you get a gold star for being polite. Of course, it's good to get on with people, but don't be a mug when obstacles are in your way.

Don't stop. Why people are scared of a Pit Bull is that when it attacks it doesn't stop. The only way to make it stop is to practically kill it. Whatever quest *you* undertake, adopt a Pit Bull mentality. Don't let anyone or anything stop you.

Inside you is a fearsome energy – unleash it, let it out; don't hold back. Atomic force is the strongest force in the universe; use it to demolish all your fears, weaknesses and timidity. Build what you need to build and destroy what you need to destroy. Don't care about good, bad, or any place in-between.

Street Olympian

Let me give you an example of the difference between sport and street: Some years ago, a top-level 800m runner, who was also a part-time policeman, came across a shop robbery in progress. The teenage perpetrator, on noticing that he'd been seen by a cop, did a runner. Now, you'd expect that our policemen would have been able to catch the young robber, but he couldn't - no matter how he tried he just couldn't collar the kid. In a competition on an athletics track the cop would easily outrun the teenager. A top 800m runner can run 400m in 45-47seconds, it's *extremely* unlikely that any kid could match that. *Here's the difference*…the street kid was a product of his terrain; agile and clever like a wild-animal. He utilised his environment, jumping over walls, zipping up stairs, getting through gaps; under things and over things - taking advantage of *his* surroundings. [Note: If you take on someone in their terrain you are automatically at a disadvantage. It is easier to win if you are playing to your strengths and their weaknesses]

Never confuse your ability in the sports arena, boxing-ring, club, track, gym and so on, with your ability on the street. Of course, there is a cross-over but it only goes so far. For instance, you may be a fast runner but what happens if someone gives you a dead-leg? Your 'strength' will be neutralised in an instant. If you abide by rules and codes in a street fight you will be taken by surprise by a jackal who has no rules or notions of fair play. In a real street fight, hit first, hit hard, stay on your feet and be prepared to run if you are overwhelmed.

It is not easy to define the qualities needed to be a Street Olympian - there are multiple scenarios that pan out on the street and life which will catch out even the most able person. However, being strong, athletic, brave, courageous and intelligent are qualities that can only be good. Being stupid, weak, afraid and cowardly are qualities which will result in you becoming a victim of the bully, boss, or any shit person or situation that passes your way.

Sport is a competition with rules. Life is a competition with no rules or different rules. No doubt our cop thought he could catch anyone, but real life isn't an athletics track.

Us vs Them

You are at war with forces that want to turn you into one of them. These forces are everywhere. They want you to become part of their Zombie Nation. They want you to lie down so they can walk all over you. Politicians try to control you by writing laws and enforcing them through the police and the legal system, which is ironic as the legal system is corrupt and the police-force has more criminals than the Mafia.

Be wary of anyone in a uniform, as soon as a person wears a uniform they start acting like a prick on a power trip. However, these people are weak, they get their strength from what they're wearing – if you have no respect for their uniform, ignore what they say and fight back, their courage disappears like a fart in a hurricane.

Part of being a warrior is that you fight for your individual freedom and liberty. It is better to die free than to live the life of a slave.

There are so many rules and regulations that normal behaviour is against the law. If you're in a street gang you may have minor skirmishes against gangs from other estates and areas, but open your eyes and you'll see that your real enemy isn't the kid in another postcode, that's bullshit; your enemies are the forces that want to bleed you dry of your individuality and replace you with a robot. They want to knock you down, pick you up, and knock you down again until you can't take it anymore, then you'll do anything they say.

In an instant you and your brothers can reverse this by deciding how you want your lives to be, and having the courage to stand firm against others. When you live by your own codes and rules and don't care what others think, you are free – but it's inevitable you will clash with the individuals and authorities who think they have a right to tell you how you should live your life. If you are fucking them off you are doing something right. Relish the fight and enjoy the battle! Your future is in your hands not theirs.

CHALLENGE - Every day for the next seven days find a stupid rule or regulation and go out of your way to break it. You will most likely find there are no consequences as there is no one around to enforce the rule; they are relying on you to do what you're told even when they're not present because they regard you as docile sheep. If someone in a uniform tells you to take a hike, ignore them – they're scared of you. The more you break nonsensical rules and regulations the less timid you become and the less you fear the consequences of not doing what you're told.

Responsible people will say that breaking rules for no reason is mindless, "the rules are there for your protection and benefit". Reject this; they are the mindless, they are the clones who go along with everything they're told to do. You are doing this *on purpose* to vaccinate yourself against zombiefication. This is far from mindless - it's because you *have a mind* that you agitate and shake up their bullshit. Additionally, breaking a rule every now and then makes you feel alive.

Remember - when people in power have control over you in the big things, they'll start trying to control you in the little things. Don't let them.

The Street Scientist

Gang fit isn't bothered with conventions or what's considered normal - it's not interested in what the majority are doing or think is right. As soon as you go along with the majority opinion *just because* it's the majority opinion, then your mind has stopped working. You really learn what's what through experience, trial and error, and the application of your brain.

The reason why adults are more stupid than ever is they've been educated to accept the status quo; but the status quo hardly benefits them - they're brain-dead. They live a life either oblivious to, or not bothered about what's really going on around them, yet the stupid fuckers complain when the price of petrol goes up or when they have to pay more tax. In a way they deserve it, their brains have atrophied to the point where they resemble walnuts. If you want to be 'comfortable' stay with the status quo and steer clear of anything which necessitates discomfort – you won't have too many problems. But you think that anyone who's achieved anything of meaning has been comfortable doing it?

Your mind is like a muscle - it gets weaker if it's not used.

The forces, laws, and dynamics which impact your life are just as important as the forces which keep the Earth revolving around the Sun. It benefits you to understand these forces. You have to break out of your conditioning and start experimenting. The street is your laboratory. Unlike the average Joe, the street scientist takes nothing at face value and questions what they're being told.

There are some great books you can learn from written by philosophers, artists, famous leaders and warriors, so allow yourself to be 'brainwashed' by great people, not idiots. Again, this is not something which is taught at school or university because, despite what they say, they are not teaching you to think for yourself. They are only teaching you to think within a subset of possible thought.

To the Street Scientist everything is an experiment and the world is full of possibilities. In the world of the Street Scientist a 'non-entity' like you can become a king.

Fear

People are employed because they're scared. In fact, they're terrified, and the longer they're employed the more terrified they become. This is strange as people seem confident, happy, and secure in their jobs. Some of these long-timers even think that because they've been employed for a long time, this gives them some sort of the right to tell you what to do; "I worked hard...blah, blah"; "Money doesn't grow on trees…blah, blah"; "You've got to earn your way…blah, blah". Don't be taken in by this, beneath their shell of arrogance and know-it-all-ness is a deep pit of unacknowledged fear. Fear so deep it's kept them a slave for years. Fear so deep that it has obliterated their childhood dreams and ambitions.

Being fearful means you can be manipulated and told what to do. Being fearful means you only live half a life. Some people stay scared all their lives; the fuckers might as well be dead.

No kid with a brain wants a job – they want to play the piano, be a dancer, drive a F1 racing car, be a scientist, a big criminal, or work with animals, *but they don't want a job*. What you're going to have to do is make your ambition your Plan A; a job should be your Plan B. Don't bother telling your teachers, careers advisor, or even your parents, they might go along with you superficially in the way someone pets a poodle, but eventually they'll say you've got to be realistic and find a job. Remember, most people don't care about your personal happiness, only that you fit into a lifestyle which pleases them.

There's nothing wrong with work, but work for free and make money from play.

Don't Waste Your Time Doing Shit

Anything you don't want to do is the definition of shit. Pure and simple.

Problem: If you spend your days doing stuff you don't want to do, your life will turn to shit. Look closely at the individuals who don't like their jobs, you can sense depression in their appearance and attitude. It's like they're broadcasting "I'm a loser - I hate my life". *If you hate what you're doing, stop doing it!*

When you're young, dopey adults tell you that if you want to get on in life you'll have to "live in the real world" – what does that even mean? The real world as they know it? Oh, the real world of paying bills and working the 9 to 5 for a living? The real world of passing your exams so you can get a good job? The real world of having to do all your shopping at the weekend along with all the other zombies? The real world of being depressed every Sunday because you've got work on Monday?
Don't take any notice of what someone says about the real world; there are a million real worlds. Choose the one in your head and go towards it – that's the only world that matters. The only delusion lies in believing it will be easy.

Many people spend their day doing stuff they *have to do* rather than things they *want to do*. You are young; you can see that doesn't make sense. Adults are so brainwashed that they have lost the ability to think clearly; they really think that spending their entire working lives doing shit is somehow necessary. Look at anyone who has become successful in life – did they get there by doing stuff they didn't want to do? Of course not. So why listen to losers who say "be realistic, in life you have to do things you don't want to do". Why would ANYONE give advice like that? They're sick.

Super Strength

Super-strength describes extreme strength by humans beyond what is believed to be normal. The most common examples are of people lifting cars to rescue a loved one or when people are in life-or-death situations.

In one case in Virginia in 2015 Eric Heffelmire was working in the family garage on a GMC pick-up truck when the jack propping up the car slipped and pinned him to the ground, with leaking petrol instantly catching fire. His 19yr old, 5ft 6in, 120lb, daughter, Charlotte immediately ran over and lifted the car off his shoulder before nearby propane tanks caught alight. Eric recalled; "I felt the weight shift, and I said, 'you almost got it,' and suddenly I'm pulled out…it was some crazy strength".
In Colorado in 1995, a police officer arrived at a car accident where a Chevy had ended up on top of a baby girl and was sinking into mud. The officer lifted the car, and the mother pulled the girl out.

There are various theories as to how normal people can summon up crazy moments of strength during emergencies, mostly centred on adrenaline, dopamine and other hormones or neurotransmitters which mobilise the body for extreme functioning, whilst decreasing pain sensation and increasing single-point focus and tunnel-vision. Gang Fit, however, isn't really interested in theories - only experience, what works, and the end effect. If normal people can momentarily become super-human, what primal, wild forces lie beneath our everyday lives?

Legendary strength coach Vladimir Zatsiorsky describes three levels of strength.

The highest is your *absolute strength*, which is the theoretical maximum that your muscle fibres, tendons, ligaments and bones can take. In theory, this can never be exceeded.

The lowest is your *maximal strength*, which is the maximum you could lift using conscious effort in a gym or other controlled environment. According to Zatsiorsky, the maximal strength of most ordinary people is about two-thirds of their absolute strength. This means that for a person who can lift 200 kilos, 300 kilos is their frame's theoretical maximum.

Somewhere between maximal strength and absolute strength is a middle ground that appears when the body goes into competitive mode. The fight or flight response also appears when faced with the pressure of competing. Zatsiorsky has measured some athletes reaching as high as 92% of their body's absolute strength during the most intense competitions.

Examples of super-strength show we can generate physical or psychological forces far greater than we think we can. Even Zatsiorsky's model doesn't explain it. If you are young, disaffected, fucked-off, poor, weak, trapped, enslaved or generally dissatisfied with life, there is a fearsome primal force just below the surface. When you start tapping into it, your life changes. Don't give a shit about anything else.

Berserker

This sounds ridiculous but it's true – I read in a newspaper that a family's pet cat went berserk. It went so wild that the entire family had to lock themselves in a bedroom. A pet cat! Animals are dangerous not only because they have weapons such as claws, horns, teeth and hooves but also because once they blow a fuse they have nothing which holds them back. No feelings of remorse, compassion or guilt. Who knows what drove the cat berserk? Maybe the final straw was its owners running out of catnip?

The English word berserk is derived from the Norse word *ber-serkr*, a term for a particular cohort of Viking warrior. 'Ber-serk' may mean 'bear shirt' or 'bare-chested', no one is quite sure. The berserkers were said to have fought like enraged wild animals, impervious to pain. From Wikipedia – 'It is proposed by some authors that the berserkers drew their power from the bear and were devoted to the bear-cult which was once widespread across the northern hemisphere. In battle, the berserkers were subject to fits of frenzy. They would howl like wild beasts, foamed at the mouth, and gnawed the iron rim of their shields. According to belief, during these fits they were immune to steel and fire, and made great havoc in the ranks of the enemy. When the fever abated they were weak and tame'.

Who knows? Perhaps the fuckers were on drugs? Anyway, the point is that even when a pet cat goes berserk it becomes a beast.

There may be occasions in life when you are completely outnumbered with no hope of escape. The individuals may want to stomp on your head until your brains are splattered on the floor. You will have to summon up every ounce of primal rage to have any chance of staying alive.

The thing about berserkers is that nothing holds them back – they cause maximum damage without hesitation. Most people don't want to physically harm other people, it goes against every fibre of who they are. That's all well and good, but in times of war they will be smashed up by people who are prepared to harm, or even enjoy causing harm. So, normally you should be cool, but if necessary you should be prepared to fight fire with greater fire. Be prepared to cause damage. It's not pretty, but your life may depend on it.

It may only be once in your life, but you will *have to* be prepared to fight like a berserker. There's no point holding back against malevolently violent people.

Create Problems

In a way, young people terrify adults. Not because they are terrifying, but because they represent the unknown and uncontrolled; an elemental force that is indifferent to adult values. They have an outlook and attitude which has withered in their elders.

Many teenagers are sick and tired of listening to the constant jabber about employment, careers, education, university, and so on. That is not really what they want. Adults, teachers and politicians are recommending this route, but the backdrop of wage-slavery, commuting, lack of money, plus the sheer dullness of most adults, shows to them this approach doesn't work. Adding to their dissonance, they are bombarded with media images of wealth, music, celebrity, sports stars and success.

If *you* are young, disconnected from the mainstream, have 'an attitude problem', or are just fed up with the daily confirmation that life is failing to live up to your youthful imaginations, you need to start creating massive 'problems' for yourself. Quit your job, drop half your friends, put yourself in frightening situations, leave your neighbourhood, whatever; because you only evolve and improve by having problems, challenges, and tests. This is why people from comfortable backgrounds, and who've had everything given to them on a plate, can't teach you shit.

If your life has no challenges apart from dragging yourself out of bed to go to some mind-numbing job on a Monday morning, you need to purposely become 'insane' – other people will think you've lost your marbles. All great people are a little insane in the sense that they have energy and visions beyond the normal zombie commuter.

Start creating problems, as a life with no problems or extraordinary challenges means you'll stay like a tiny half-human.

Jump Off a Building

Some time ago, whilst walking down a busy street in South London, I noticed a kid jump onto the pavement from the 1st floor balcony of a block of flats. It looked cool and no doubt saved him time in not having to use the stairs or the lift. Someone with weak legs would have crumpled. Can you imagine an old, fat or unfit individual doing this? They would have killed themselves.

The kid didn't roll on landing to lessen the impact, he just used his legs as shock absorbers in a squatting action, then straightened up and walked off.

Develop and retain the ability to tolerate acute physical stress; this is what most adults have lost - they can no longer cope with shocks or extremes.

So what qualities do you need to be able to jump from a height? Strong legs of course, but also a strong back and core - an overall robust physique. Your legs need to be resilient enough to absorb the shock. It's better to be lighter and strong rather than heavy. You need to be flexible - a stiff object which isn't strong, snaps (babies and young people can come out of bad tumbles virtually unscathed for this reason. Old age is the reverse; weak, inflexible and brittle).

People are taught to dissipate the landing forces by rolling on landing, which is all well and good but not the point. The point is you should develop the *qualities* which enable you to jump off a building, take it in your stride, and come off unscathed.

Start off jumping from low walls, six feet high or so, and gradually work your way up; first on grass then on a hard surface. You'll find out your psychological and physical limits.

Note: when you're up high the ground seems further down than it actually is because your eye-level is five or more feet higher. Either crouch down on the wall to reduce the perceived height or get used to mentally discounting the extra 'phantom' height.

Cowardice

Looking and acting like a tough guy but failing to deliver when push comes to shove, makes you look like an idiot. Cowardice can't be covered up, everyone will see it. Being tough doesn't mean that you win everything, that's impossible – taking a few beatings yourself is part of street life; once you've taken some you get used to it, they are a necessary part of your evolution as a warrior. Being strong isn't about never being beaten, but not being afraid to commit when the going gets tough. At a low level, fearful people will be put off by someone who looks tough - so looking the part will make you come out tops with a minimum amount of effort. At another level however, looking tough will not be a deterrent to others…in fact it may attract those who want to pit themselves against you.

The 'pain' of being a coward lasts longer than the pain of a black-eye or a few bruises. Get this into your head – being tough isn't about coming out on top all of the time. We all lose and we all fail, that is a completely normal part of life. What is tough is sticking to your principles and standing firm in the face of danger.

Note: Real violence (not the average street scrap) is *very* nasty, try and avoid it. Hit first, hit fast, hit hard, then get out. If you can't you will have to fight like an animal. It's not nice, but you will have to be prepared to inflict damage or incapacitate the aggressor. You may still lose, but there is no true courage, bravery or heroism without risk.

High Intensity Interval Training (HIIT)

The clue is in the word 'intensity' – if these sessions aren't hard, you are doing them wrong. But the intensity is appropriate to distance or time in that it's maximal effort *over the session*. In other words, the earlier reps are sub-max (only slightly, don't be a chicken), but as the session progresses each rep gets harder to achieve at the target pace. Over the session your heart rate, fatigue and willingness to live increases in a peaks and troughs or 'rachet' fashion.

If you push yourself you should be DOA (almost) at the end of the final repetition.

Generally, a HIIT session involves acidosis/oxygen debt; 6 x 200m with 3 mins between doesn't involve all-out sprinting but a high sub-max. Pure sprint sessions involve fast (95% or higher of top speed) short reps with long recoveries where there is no acidosis, or at least a good recovery between reps.

Some sessions to try (on track, road or grass). These are running sessions, use your imagination to convert to your sport or activity.

1/ Sprint 200m (or 30secs) as fast as you can - rest for three minutes and repeat. Session is finished when you have completed six runs

2/ Run 400m (or 70secs) non-stop - rest for five minutes. Repeat three times

3/ 400m - five times with 1 min between

3/ 300m fast (or 45secs) - rest for 90 seconds then sprint 150m (around 20secs). Rest for five minutes. Repeat twice

4/ 10 x 100m; 1 min between

5/ 18 x 60m; split into 3 sets. 1 min btwn reps; 8 min btwn sets

6/ 100m (3mins recovery); 150m (4 mins); 200m (8mins); 200 (8mins); 150m (6mins); 100m

7/ 600m x 3 (8 mins btwn)

8/ 8 x 300m; split into 2 sets. 4 mins btwn reps; 10 mins btwn sets

9/ 40m, 60m, 80m, 100m, 120m, 150m – full recovery btwn

10/ Find a reasonably steep hill. Run up for 150m. Slowly walk down (3/4mins). The session is over when you've completed six runs

11/ 100/150m hill – run up fast; jog for 15secs at the top (on flat) – sprint 100m. Repeat four times.

Once you've done these you'll realize the difference between jogging and hard work. Jogging does naff all, only zombies waste time on it.

Anger Is an Energy

John McEnroe was a genius tennis player of the 1970s and 80s. He said the angrier he got the better he played. If he was losing, he got angry. When a point went against him, he got angry. When he believed the umpire had made a dodgy line call, he got angry. When the crowd booed him, he got angry.

People say it's not good to get angry. Well, if your anger makes you do something stupid which you'll regret, then it's negative. But if your anger spurs you on to achieve something 'impossible' then it's positive. In reality, *anger is neither positive nor negative, it is an energy.* It is fuel, it is nitro-glycerine. It has the ability to destroy or the ability to create. Even the destruction bit can be positive in that destroying something which shits on your life is positive.

People who are telling you not to get angry are trying to control you. It's perfectly acceptable to be angry at being a weak, penniless zombie. It's a good thing. You want to use any emotion or mindset which changes your situation and creates something massive. Changing your life is *the* most important thing you can do. It also enables you to help other people (if that's what you want) in far more effective ways than if you're weak with no power or resources.

1/ Being angry with yourself helps you change. The usual bullshit is to be proud of who you are, but if you're an overweight pathetic slave who writes bad poetry, what have you got to be proud of? Be fucking angry, be very angry – don't accept it. Why should you be proud of yourself if you're a useless piece of crap and no good for anybody?

2/ Being angry with other people is good if they constantly bring negativity to your door. Be angry with them. Leave them behind. You won't go to heaven just because you're nice to jerks.

3/ Channel your anger (not get rid of it) and use it to propel you in the direction you really want. Use it as a deflective force-field to defend you from all the circumstances and situations that knob-heads and authorities use to try and rule you.

Ritalin Boy

I was at a school where almost half of the kids were on some sort of drug to calm them down - apparently, they had Attention Deficit Hyperactivity Disorder (ADHD), a term invented by expert fuckers who don't realise it's quite natural for some kids not to like being confined to a classroom listening to a boring teacher.

Most of these kids were being given Ritalin (prescribed by doctors with the approval of the parents), the name for a drug which turns a normal exuberant kid into a mind-numbed zombie. One particular kid was given Ritalin every morning as soon as he arrived at school, so *before lunch* he was brain-dead zombie, as quiet as a mouse with no interaction, but *after lunch*, once the drug had worn off, he was very lively, chucking things around the classroom and not taking any notice of the teacher; having a laugh and not really learning anything. Anyway, one summer the class he was in went on a week's sailing and kayaking course on the River Thames; if you don't know it, the Thames is a polluted and muddy river which meanders through London, cutting it in half.

Note: Learning to sail a yacht is not a straightforward affair. How to adjust the sails, rudder and daggerboard with reference to the current, wind strength and direction, takes a while to pick up. There are more things to control and get used to than most people realise.

Guess who picked it up the quickest and became the most proficient at sailing after one week? You guessed it, 'Ritalin Boy'. At the end of the week the sailing centre gave him a certificate for outstanding student. He outperformed the kids who were A grade at maths, A grade at science, and A grade at being the teacher's pet. In a different environment Ritalin Boy became A grade.

If you judge a gorilla on how well it can swim it will be a failure all its life. The experts in a society based on swimming will then classify the gorilla as having some sort of syndrome or disorder, and pump it full of drugs to fit in.

If you are like Ritalin Boy, don't let the teachers denigrate you, don't let society convince you that you are abnormal, and most of all *don't take the fucking drugs*.

School is only trying to turn you into the sort of individual who does well at school. Your real life starts when school ends.

Off Grid

The answer to being trapped in the Rat Race is not to be like Grizzly Adams and live off-grid. If you don't know, 'The Life and Times of Grizzly Adams' is the story of a man who flees to the Californian wilderness (after being wrongly accused of murder) and has sex with a bear. It's seems idyllic to live out in the middle of nowhere, but it's tougher than it looks and you'll live an unnecessarily hard life if you completely drop out. Plus, the world is huge, full of incredible things to see and experience – you want to see it, no?

The real off grid is using or taking the parts of the grid you want, whilst disregarding the rest, in other words *not being trapped* in the grid; using it for your own ends. Wherever you live all you need is a smart phone, a laptop and an internet connection - with this you can potentially connect with billions of people and make money. When people do a Grizzly Adams these days, they take the internet with them, this gives them the best of both worlds; hyper-connected when they need it and isolated from society's shit when they want it.

If you live in the City the opportunities are virtually unlimited, maybe you can't see it because you're blind to it, but it's true. What you shouldn't do is allow yourself to be caught up in the rat race, doing the 9 to 5 and turning into a moron. Don't believe anyone, being a wage-slave is not a fulfilling life

When you have one bank account, one passport, and one source of income you can be shut down by the State in an instant. You are at the mercy of the Law and the authorities. If you step out of line or say something nasty on social media they can control you or 'starve you to death'. This is what happened to the indigenous Native Americans in the US; they relied on the American Buffalo (Bison) for food and clothing. Foreign fuckers arrived and proceeded to kill 100's of millions of the Bison, literally starving the natives to death. They were decimated.

Have at least three bank accounts, have digital cash, cryptocurrency and hard cash. Buy some gold, diamonds, land and other assets. If your parents are from another country see if you can apply for passport, or live in another country and see if you can apply for a passport there. Some countries may give you a passport if you have a shit load of money. This may seem far off to you at present, but all it is saying is that diversification gives you options in case of trouble. It will be difficult for someone to control you, cut off your source of income or savings, or stop you travelling by confiscating your passport.

This is using the vast network of the grid for your own ends - the only point of the Grid. You control it, it doesn't control you.

Human Marshmallow

No living creature in the history of the world has had a default setting of physical comfort. So, if all you want is physical comfort you are denying life. Older adults like to be comfortable; they avoid hard physical work; "It hurts!" Slowly they become softer and more fragile, less able to cope. If you've got your eyes open you've already seen that for yourself. It's frightening.

Much of modern life is aimed at saving you energy whilst at the same time oversupplying you with energy in the form of calories. In the Wild, practically the reverse is the case. To get energy (food) you have to expend energy. Further, you may expend energy and not get any…for a while, or you may get some, just not enough. This is an extremely important distinction; one you need to get into your brain – *every creature on the planet needs to 'exercise' to get food. The food isn't delivered to them on a plate.*

Comfort and conserving energy certainly has its place, but modern life wants to turn you into a human marshmallow, with labour-saving devices and access to abundant food. It's easy to be seduced into expending less and less effort in everyday life, so you need to fight against it.

An anti-marshmallow routine for life:

45% Resistance training
45% Intervals (short to long)
1-2% Mega-challenges
8% Randomness

These percentages are *general* targets for the amount of energy or time you should spend in each area.

Included in the 'randomness' section is the idea of mini-challenges – basically, the everyday two-fingers up to the environment which is trying to slowly kill you by giving you too much comfort. Walking up escalators, taking the stairs instead of lifts, using push-doors not automatic ones, not taking the junk food and high-sugar freebies which are offered to you...on and on. You might think this isn't important – but if you don't want to end up like the marshmallows around you, you have to do the opposite of what they do.

Get used to high intensity training. Seek out stress - cold, heat, starvation, exhaustion and giant exercise sessions...get to know yourself. Run fast without stopping - your heart will be pumping so hard you'll feel like it's going to burst. Cycle downhill as fast as you can, almost out of control. How long can you keep your hand in a flame? Test your limits, push your limits - then you can cope with shit which normal people shy away from.

Settle for physical comfort when you're in your coffin.

"There Is Always Tomorrow"

No there isn't

One day you're going to die.
You don't know when you're going to die.
There are opportunities which may arise only once.

The idea that you can put off until tomorrow what you should attend to today has created more misery and regret than just about anything else. If you think like this you will never get anything done. Plans unrealised, goals never reached, ambitions unfulfilled.

Now is the time to assess yourself and the direction you are heading. What does it look like? We are always being told to be nice to ourselves, not to be too self-critical, after all "we're only human". Nothing can come from this. In this instance you *should* be harsh on yourself, don't listen to your own bullshit. Be sick with yourself for always saying "I'll start it tomorrow". Your life should be a progression - you can't progress if you always defer things; weeks turn to months, months turn to years. So, whatever 'insane' plans, incredible dreams, or life transforming ideas you have, start them now. Don't care what other people think and don't be put off by the fear of failure.

"Begin with the end in mind" is the usual advice. We haven't managed to cheat death yet - the ultimate end is that you will die. Everyone you know will die. Everything you know, everything you do, everyone you love; all your successes and all your mistakes will turn to dust. With this stark ending in mind what is the point of timidity, lack of confidence and fear? Stake your claim during your brief spell here. Live big, live gloriously, live well, because sooner or later it will all come to an end.

When we have an externally imposed deadline, we sometimes surprise ourselves how much we get done, how focused we are and how much energy we have. The problem is that we have our own long-term goals and ambitions but they are open-ended with no deadlines. There is no tangible penalty for not achieving them. This is why you need to be tough on yourself. Create a psychological imperative because you really don't have all the time in the world.

There is no way on Earth you will fulfill one iota of your potential if you have the attitude that there is always tomorrow. This is the only chance you get at life – don't fuck it up.

Food

In your quest for health and strength what you eat shouldn't be ignored. You may think you can get away with eating muck but you can't, your body will eventually turn to shit. Young people think they are immortal, impervious to the things that afflict older people, without seeming to comprehend that all older people were like them once.
This is something you *must* get into your walnut brain – if you don't do anything thing different, you will end up like the older people around you. If that's what you want, fine – end up a boring, pathetic twat with no energy.

You cannot be a strong independent person if your body is slowly decaying, so you need to look after it, not wait until the signs of ill-health start showing up. Meat, fish, eggs and vegetables should be the main elements of your diet along with some starch foods such as potatoes and rice. If you're going to the gym it's ok to take a protein drink after your workout. If you get this right you can have some crap every now and then – just don't make the crap a big part of your diet.

A teenage kid I know decided to change his diet; he swapped the usual junk in his lunchbox with fish, cheese and an apple, or something similar. Here's what happened: He got ridiculed by his class mates, the morons who had crisps, chocolate bars, sandwiches, processed stuff and cans of soda in their lunchboxes. "Why are you eating that shit?!" "You're a weirdo!" Just imagine, the lobotomized morons thought what they were eating was normal and that my mate's diet was abnormal, can you believe that? He told me about this at the athletics track when we were sprint training; it was no surprise to me – once you step outside the mainstream and do your own thing you get ridiculed by the brain-dead. It always happens.

Meat, fish, eggs and vegetables are your 'health foods'. They are normal. They are what humans have been eating for a million years. Anyone who ridicules you for eating well is an owned zombie…victim to the forces that want to push junk food down your throat and make you ill for the sake of profit.

Some people think it's not cool to look after your own health – they would rather 'enjoy themselves' and not worry about it. *Listen* – you do not enjoy being overweight and unhealthy. You do not enjoy being so physically shit that you can no longer climb up a flight of stairs without having a heart attack. You do not enjoy losing all the health benefits of youth and vitality because you ate pizza and crisps all your life. There are so many physical, metabolic and psychological problems associated with being unhealthy and unwell, that it would take a whole book to write about them.

In your quest to conquer the planet you should eat well. This alone will put you in the top 5% of the population.

TEST – Survive without food and dominate hunger. As Gang Fit has stated earlier, physical strength without mental strength is useless. It goes without saying that you need food to live but many adults are fucked-up by food addictions and cravings. Why would you intentionally 'starve' yourself? Look at it this way – why would you do a test or challenge which was easy? To improve, to grow and to get stronger, you have to do stuff that is challenging. Too many kids are crying and moaning because they can't have their favourite candy bar or go to McDonalds. Food controls them so they become victims to chocolate, sweets, pizzas, cakes. These losers have weak minds and no self-control. Go for 24 hours without food – just water, tea or coffee. No juices, sodas or drinks containing sugar. I didn't eat for 5 days – now, not eating for a day is laughably easy. Break your connection with food *and* your reliance on anything.

Boomerang

"Mummy, I want to climb the big tree". "No, it's too dangerous".
"Mummy, I want to be an astronaut when I grow up". "Don't be silly. That's not for the likes of you".
"Mummy, look! I can fly like a bird!" "No you can't!"
"Mummy, I'm scared". "Don't be a baby".
"Mummy, I want to be a singer". "What?! With your voice?!"
"Mum, can you help me with my school work?" "I'm too busy"

"Mum, can you tell me how you and dad met". "Shhh, I'm watching TV".
"Mum, have you got £5?" "No. You think money grows on trees?"
"Mum, I didn't mean to…I'm sorry". "That's not good enough. You're always causing trouble".

Mother – "Why do you never take any notice of me or your dad?" You - "What the hell?! I'm going out".

Them - "What have we done to deserve this?"

Fuck that shit

If your parents have fucked you up, join the gang. There are so many useless parents that it's practically the norm. But it's no good for you to dwell on it – don't let them fuck you up when they're not even around. Some people are so messed up by their parents, they never get over it, they're stay fucked up until they die. Real parents let their kids be themselves, encourage them and help them flourish; useless parents don't care about their kids.

If you don't get on with your parents, it's ok; don't think you'll be rewarded in heaven for liking people who are idiots. Parents don't have special powers, they are like anyone else, some are good, some are useless – get on with forging your life. If they are good parents they will come through for you in some way. If they don't, move on.

Fucked-Up-Ness

A short note on do-gooders - steer clear of them, their need to do good is a pathological disorder. The idea that you should be nice to everyone, put others first, be reasonable, turn the other cheek, help out and so on, is truly fucked up. Leave people to their own lives. The sort of people who are always running around helping others are parasites, feeding off how "wonderful and caring" they are. It makes them feel big. Furthermore, these idiots will try and rope you into wasting *your time* sorting out other people's problems.

There will always be miserable people, people on shit-street, people with problems, people with disabilities, people with cancer, retarded people, fat people, stupid people, people who support Arsenal – you can't spend your life helping them.

Half the time do-gooders make things worse - "I was only trying to help" is their response when everything goes tits up. Putting everyone else first is a sure recipe for a miserable life. Help the people you want to help and ignore the ones you don't.

Exploitation

People exploit you because you have '*Exploit* Me' written on your forehead.

The reason you earn shit is because you deserve shit. The reason you have no money is because you deserve no money. The reason people take advantage of you is because you deserve to be taken advantage of. Does this mean you are useless? No it doesn't. It only means that you have low expectations of yourself. You have no confidence and self-belief. Unless you were born rich and went to a top school, you will most likely have been brought up with limited thinking. Now you have to turn that around and stop being a wanker. Start expecting more from life. It is highly unlikely that you will rise higher than your expectations, so make your expectations far higher than they are now.

A few years back an interesting study was carried out; the same job vacancy was advertised but with two different levels of pay – the stated wage in one of the adverts was far lower than the other. Incredibly, more people applied for the lower wage vacancy even though the position and experience required were identical. You would think that more people would apply for the higher paid job wouldn't you? It goes against commonsense. But this is far from surprising – many people don't think they are good enough to receive over a certain amount of money. They are scared of it. They have psychological limits.

If someone offered you $800 or $100 an hour for help or advice, which one would you accept? Someone with confidence would have no problem taking the higher amount. Would you? It takes a while for someone to go from zero to hero, but you have to start asking for and expecting more. Eventually you will look back and wonder why the hell you sold yourself so short.

I was taking an Uber to some crap part of south-east London dominated by Albanian drug gangs and fried chicken shops. I got talking to the driver, a guy from Morocco. He said his close and extended family had moved to southern Spain years earlier (before he had moved to London) and that one day, when his kids grew up, he would go live with them. As well as being an uber driver, he said he did odd jobs here and there to make ends meet. What he told me next was an example of why he was poor even though he worked hard. Around twenty years ago, an old school friend of his opened a clinic in London doing aesthetic treatments for rich women – botox, overpriced rejuvenating creams…all that shit. He did so well at this that he opened up another one in Italy. After a while his friend became a millionaire. One day he asked our uber driver if he would spend the day on the door at the London clinic, sort of like a concierge; his friend was organising a special day and wanted to impress potential clients. That all went well, and at the end of the day his friend gave him £200 for his help.

Here's the crazy part – our uber driver gave him £100 *back* and said one hundred was fine, he was just "helping a friend".

What sort of bullshit is that?

The driver had told me this because he was genuinely impressed with the achievements of his school friend, and was recounting a story to while away the time until we arrived at fried chicken land. Unfortunately for him his story backfired, I spent the next fifteen minutes telling him why he was a jerk. "He was only being nice!" Nice to whom? His millionaire friend? Two hundred quid represents loose change to him. A bloke with two children to bring up, and a wife at home, turns down money offered in good faith by a millionaire? Stupid fucker – he deserves to stay poor.

If you are poor, you deserve it. Start believing in yourself.

Note: There are people around you who bring you down, who are negative about your talents and abilities. Apparently, they tell you for "your own benefit". You *have* to get rid of these individuals. Leave them behind. When you start achieving things, either by yourself or with your band of brothers, it's like a veil has lifted. You lose your low expectations of what you think you deserve.

King of the Hill

No matter how much running (on the flat) or fitness training an individual has done, running hills is a shock to the system. Nothing is written in stone but it is better for you to have a reasonable amount of fitness before undertaking serious hill training. If you have no real fitness (how did that happen?) and you foolishly try a mega-hill session, not only will you not be able to finish the session, but you'll most likely vomit.

A well-trained runner can run very, very close to max on each rep without sacrificing the quality of the following rep (dependent on the length of recovery between reps), less fit individuals would have to pace themselves. Indeed, a sign of fitness is the ability to recover quickly after intense effort. You can 'hurt' yourself on each rep, and survive. The last rep is all out war. In a sense the last rep is psychologically easier as it 'takes care of itself' – it doesn't matter if you near kill yourself on the last rep, you have no recovery interval to observe. You can lie down for as long as you like. It's intense, but you get used to it.

My hill sessions were brutal, each rep basically finishing DOA. Sometimes my quads would start to cramp near the top of the hill. One fellow in our group was taken to hospital – he wasn't fit enough. After a few months off hills I completed a session in the evening with my friends; for hours after my pulse rate was racing, I had a headache and couldn't sleep. I phoned my best friend because I thought I was going to die. The next week all was fine.

Hill training really benefits from doing with others. If you and your mates have any competitiveness or pride – you will all run faster. It is psychologically harder because you know the session is going to be tough, but psychologically easier in that you share the pain, plus others in the group can take turns to lead. If someone is much faster than the rest, they will always be leading, that's not good for them or you. It's preferable to have a group where abilities are quite close. Run hard, hill sessions are fearsome; the more fearsome, and the more you overcome it, the better the feeling is.

When the strength drains from your legs, when you can no longer initiate strong muscular contractions - if you lose focus and stop purposely pushing yourself, it's very easy to slow down. So, an aggressive mindset is essential. A hard hill session is both exhilarating and frightening, but when you've completed a tough session, there's no better feeling. Your training mates are your band of brothers. People say sport is fake war, maybe it is, but proper hill training is war. Last man standing. If you are not prepared to hurt yourself – go home and stop fucking about.

Tip: When you find yourself slowing down near the top, rather than trying to push and extend your stride, do the opposite, consciously shorten you stride and move your arms quicker; this will increase your cadence, make you feel lighter and increase your speed (for a while) – the equivalent of shifting to an easier gear when cycling up a hill.

A hard hill session only needs to be done once a week; twice a week if you're not doing anything else. Every 3rd or 4th hill session don't do a warm-up. No cheating, run the first rep full-pelt, otherwise it would essentially be a warm-up. Without a warm-up your body has to cope with a sudden extreme demand. Young humans and animals in the wild can go from rest to full pelt in the blink of an eye. It's one of the hallmarks of youth and dynamic vitality that the body can cope with sudden changes in conditions. Doing a hill session without a warm-up will *most likely* lead to a poorer session overall, the whole session will probably feel more uncomfortable especially if the rest intervals are short - but a no warm-up session is a different kind of session. Call it 'under the radar' conditioning.

****

Generally, a hill session involves acidosis and oxygen debt to a greater or lesser extent – 6 x 150m+ hills with 3 mins between doesn't involve 'all-out' sprinting but a high sub-max. Pure sprint sessions (if that is possible on a hill – we'll call it "100% effort") involve fast short reps with long recoveries where there is no acidosis, or at least, complete recovery (sort of) between reps.

Some suggestions:

1/ Find a reasonably steep hill. Run up for 150m. Slowly walk down (3/4mins). The session is over when you've completed six runs

2/ 100/150m hill – run up fast; jog for 15secs at the top (on flat) – sprint 100m. Repeat four times.

3/ 40m; 80m; 150m; 200m – slow walk back recovery. 3 sets – 8mins btwn sets

4/ 8 x 250m – 5mins btwn

5/ 50m; 100m; 150m; 200m; 150m 100m; 50m; 250m – 4 mins btwn

6/ 2 x (5 x 180m) – 4mins btwn reps. 10 mins btwn sets

7/ 6 x 280m – 6 mins btwn

8/ 50m; 100m; 50m; 100m; 50m; 100m – 4mins bwtn. Repeat after 10mins.

9/ 3 x (100m; 150m; 200m; 250m) – 4mins btwn reps. 8 mins btwn sets
10/ 3 x (4 x 150m) – 4mins btwn reps. 6 mins btwn sets

These sessions are just ideas, the design of a session is only limited by your imagination.

Timing your repetitions and rest intervals removes all doubt about your progression. You don't have to time, but timing keeps you focused when the session starts getting tough. Without timing there can be a lot of self-kiddology – your mind starts trying to bullshit you.

Your access to a suitable hill determines the nature of the hill; length, slope and surface. One could argue that flatter hills are easier, but what makes a session tough is the effort you put in. A run of 100% effort over 200m on a hill is different to 100% effort on the flat.   There is a greater vertical element (gravity) involved, demanding different muscular qualities. So, it's not just quality of effort but the nature of the effort.

Hill sessions really sort out the men from the boys.

Oobleck

Oobleck is a non-Newtonian fluid, which means it has properties of both fluids and solids. If you hit Oobleck with a hammer it becomes hard, but you can stick your finger in it like a fluid. Don't believe it? Make some for yourself – one part cornflour to 1.5 to 2 parts water.

Oobleck is a good example of how a Gang Fit individual should be. A sort of non-Newtonian individual – 'liquid' normally but solid and unyielding when required.

The real warrior is not a bully of the poor and the weak. He has honour and lives by his word, *however*, if anyone tries to cage him, abuse him, dominate him or tell him how to live his life, his fearsomeness and independence turns him into an impenetrable force-field, or if necessary, a savage tiger. Easy going generally, but utterly 'unreasonable' (what other people will say) when pushed. You *have* to be like that as always doing what other people say will destroy your life. Why would you listen to circus fleas, zombies or the enslaved? "Oh, you have to get on with people!" No, you fucking don't, who taught you that shit? You only need to get on with people you need to get with – the ones you like and love, and the ones who improve your life.

If you have a non-Newtonian mindset, your friends will see it, you'll become someone they admire as you don't fold in the face of a crisis. You support them and they will support you.

TEST – the next time someone tries to push you around, stand up to them. The *only* reason you haven't done it before is you are scared of them. They may be someone who is used to getting their own way with you, so when you refuse they will call you unreasonable, maybe cry, or even threaten you with 'consequences'. Tell them to stop their bullshit - you won't be moved. Take the consequences of this and be a man. They will learn they can no longer take you for granted. The more you do this the easier it becomes to say no to people - and stand firm. Don't let other people waste your time and energy. Don't let them dominate you.

Be like Oobleck, soft when you need to be, but hard when an idiot tries to push you around.

Develop Your Talents

The story of Wilma Rudolph who became the first American woman to win three gold medals at a single Olympic Games.

[Note: The following text from www.biography.com and www.tnhistoryforkids.org]

Early Life

Wilma Glodean Rudolph was born premature and sickly on June 23, 1940, in St. Bethlehem, Tennessee; the 20th of 22 children to parents Ed and Blanche Rudolph. The doctors doubted she would survive. She developed pneumonia and polio as a child, making her disabled for most of her childhood. For several years, her mother, brother or sister had to massage her legs four times a day. She had to wear a metal leg brace for several years. Wilma didn't start school until she was eight. Due to the intensive therapy her parents gave her she was able to permanently take off her brace by the age of nine.

Growing up in the South before segregation was outlawed, Rudolph attended an all-black school where she played on the basketball team. A naturally gifted runner, she was soon recruited to train with Tennessee State University track coach Ed Temple, and whilst still in high school, she qualified for the 1956 Summer Olympic Games in Melbourne, Australia. The youngest member of the U.S. team at the age of 16, she won a bronze medal in the sprint relay event.
After finishing high school, Rudolph enrolled at Tennessee State University, where she trained hard for the next Olympics.

Held in Rome, Italy, the 1960 Olympic Games was a golden time for Rudolph. After setting a world record of 11.3 seconds in the 100-meter dash in the semi-finals, she won the 100 in the final with a time of 11.0secs. Similarly, she broke the Olympic record in the 200-meter dash (23.2 seconds) in the semi-finals before winning the 200 in the final. She was also part of the U.S. team that beat the world record in the 4 x100-meter relay (44.4 seconds) in the Olympic semi-finals before winning the relay in the final in 44.5 seconds. Most notably, Rudolph became the first American woman to win three gold medals at a single Olympic Games. She instantly became one of the most popular athletes of the Rome Games as well as an international superstar.

Following the Games, Rudolph made numerous appearances on television and received several honours, including the Associated Press Woman Athlete of the Year Award, which she received twice, in both 1960 and 1961. She retired from competition not long after, becoming a track coach, but her accomplishments on the Olympic track remained her best known: Throughout the '60s, Rudolph was widely considered to be the world's fastest woman.

Legacy

Rudolph shared her story with the world in 1977 with her autobiography, *Wilma*. Her book was later turned into a TV film. In the 1980s, she was inducted into the U.S. Olympic Hall of Fame and she established the Wilma Rudolph Foundation to promote amateur athletics. She is remembered as one of the fastest women in track and as a source of inspiration for generations of African-American athletes. She once stated, "Winning is great, sure, but if you are really going to do something in life, the secret is learning how to lose. Nobody goes undefeated all the time. If you can pick up after a crushing defeat, and go on to win again, you are going to be a champion someday."

****

Wilma Rudolph is an example that whatever your circumstances, you can succeed; whatever your background you can succeed; whatever your colour, age or educational status - you can succeed.
There is something important though – no sprinter gets to the top of the world without having a genetic advantage over the majority of the planet. Someone without the genetics will never be a top sprinter. Rudolph concentrated on something she had a talent for – this is the magic ingredient.

Fortunately, there are a zillion more ways to be a champion than winning a gold medal at the Olympics. If you're big, build crushing strength. If you're fast, develop blinding speed. If you like fighting, take up a combat sport. If you're clever, learn astrophysics. If you're creative, be an artist. Everyone has natural tendencies and predispositions; find out what you're good at (*and like doing*) and concentrate on that. If you spend your energies on things you have a talent for, you will become world-class. Let other things take a back seat. It's also likely that in becoming world-class you will make money doing it.

Some people tell you that you need to be a balanced person or an all-rounder to succeed; apparently you need to pass exams in many subjects to increase your chances of getting a job and doing well in life – this is pure bollocks. No one gets anywhere by being 'balanced'.

The Golden Rule - to become a champion, world-class or extremely rich, concentrate on things you are good at and interest you. If money is the only thing that interests you, concentrate on making it. Some people say that only focusing on making money means you're an evil person – ignore them.

Now You See Me, Now You Don't

A few weeks before the London riots in 2012, I saw a two-page magazine advert from a well-known sports clothing company. The first page was a photo of a hoodie during the day, the second page was the same hoodie wearing dark clothes at night…practically invisible. It was pretty obvious what the company was trying to do but it backfired on the idiots – the riots called their marketing bluff. They had tried to sell an edgy image to kids but as soon as something serious actually happened they pulled the ad.

[The riots were incredible. London went on lockdown; shops closed early and were boarded up; it was like some sort of zombie apocalypse. A strange wave of tension, excitement and anarchy hit the streets. This spread to other cities.

One morning I got up early and went for a walk to check things out - random shops had had their windows smashed overnight; proof that jackals come out in the dark. Thing is, my area wasn't anywhere near the riots; proof that when some real shit happens it will spread like a virus – a self-fulfilling contagion. Society is one-step away from chaos – one day you may be trapped in it].

A friend of mine was jailed for taking part in the riots; they traced him through his DNA. You don't have to be paranoid (maybe you do) but just be careful - your business is your business. Whatever reasons they give you, your private life, dna, data, name of pet Gerbil, doesn't belong to the Government.

If you live in a town or city, you are being tracked practically everywhere you go. Cameras are filming you; the next time you are out make a point of looking for them. Some are on tops of buildings and others on lampposts. Some cameras you can see swiveling around. Why are the fuckers doing this? Apparently, it's to protect you from crime. But is crime going down? Fuck no.

The people in control have decided that it's necessary for people to be protected from themselves.

There are high-resolution satellites orbiting the planet that are recording everything. They are not actually in space, but so high up that you don't notice them – they look like small dots in the sky.

They can triangulate your position from your phone. See where you've travelled from your oyster card. Your health data is being shared. Agencies can access your phone calls, emails and texts. The police can access all your social media. Your address is on the electoral roll. Banks and finance companies share information about you with credit agencies. Passports have your biometric details. Facial recognition and full body X-rays are used at airports. Your phone is hackable. Your computer is hackable. They know the porn you've watched, the websites you've visited, and when you last went to piss.

Sooner or later everyone will be chipped (like dogs), done at birth, then everyone will be fucked. You will be chipped to make 'your life easier' - to access services, benefits, insurance, healthcare...everything. You will need to be chipped to get vaccinated and send your kids to school. You will need to be chipped to vote. You will need to be chipped to fly on planes. You will need to be chipped to enter a public building. If you're not chipped you will be deemed a criminal.

The zombies are sleepwalking into a mass surveillance society; videoed, recorded, tracked and logged. What can be done about it? Nothing. Nothing can be done about it. Not only can nothing be done about it, but the zombies will think you are weird for having a problem with it. Fuck the lot of them.

The only way this will be stopped is if there is a major disaster or aliens knock out everything electronic on the planet and send us back to the dark ages. Then, glorious chaos will ensue, and strong and clever people will rise up – that would be one hell of a time.

The previous 'off grid' section advises that the best way to deal with all this is to diversify your identity and resources, but what if you can't or haven't yet? You may be young, or poor, or previously ignorant to the potential realities of life. In truth it's highly unlikely in today's world that you can make yourself invisible, but you shouldn't be an idiot and broadcast everything. Your business is yours. In some shithole countries it's still possible to be born, live, and die with hardly anyone knowing you existed. In a developed country it's virtually impossible.

[There's a scene in the film, 'Predator' where Arnie realizes he can make himself invisible to the alien by covering himself with mud – an excellent example that if your enemy is invisible, to even the odds you have to make yourself invisible. This turned the predator's strength against itself]

1/ Don't go on the Electoral Roll (ok, so you won't be able to vote, so what – it doesn't make any difference to your outcome in life). Note: you need to be on the electoral roll to access credit. But you don't need credit, you need make money. When you've got a ton of money no one cares about you being on the electoral roll.
2/ Don't publicise your private business
3/ Pay by cash as much as possible
4/ Make sensitive agreements in person not email
5/ Have a basic 'dumb' phone as well as a smart phone

If you can't (or don't) want to do the above, you will need a 'fuck you' attitude. People who may try to threaten you by revealing things about you can take a hike. Owned people can be manipulated and blackmailed by others, not you. The most pathetic example of this are the employed, scared of what their boss may think.

If you are independent and free, no one can push you around. Don't let anyone scare you by the threat of highlighting your apparent misdemeanors. All warriors face challenges head on, they stay strong.

****

There may be occasions when you are being chased by coppers or security guards. Gang members, thugs, or adversaries may want to give you a beating. If your physical condition is poor, you will be found wanting when you need to perform, when your life and future liberty may be at stake. All animals in the wild understand this; it is literally life or death for them, if they are overwhelmed and can no longer escape, they are history.

I witnessed a young kid being chased in a shopping centre by two security guards, he gave then the runaround, it was like watching two hippos trying to catch a gazelle – the guards had no chance. They could see him but they couldn't catch him. Eventually, he made himself 'invisible' by escaping.

Strength, agility, speed and fitness are always an advantage. Don't get soft.

Muscle and Strength

In the past few years the exercise paradigm of how to most effectively lose weight, keep fit and get strong has changed - now it's believed that the best way is by undertaking short bursts of intense exercise with plenty of recovery – us sprinters knew that for decades. Rather than the fitness of the long-distance wimp, you develop the dynamic strength and physique of a sprinter, decathlete or boxer…lean strong and fast. I would take it further and suggest that life should be like that; in fact life *is* like that. You know that on the street that there are long periods of nothing with short bursts of excitement, fear and adrenalin.

[Note: This is how you build mental strength as well - periods of intense pressure or stress followed by recovery. To create or build something you need consistent application, that's true, but to harden your mindset you need to face fears and challenging situations – talking in public, facing threats of violence, smashing up zombies, whatever.]

You need regular doses of physical stress (exercise), the higher the stress the greater the stimulus to the body. With the appropriate downtime, nutrition, and sleep, your body will adapt. The right sort of exercise coupled with correct eating will boost your transformation from non-entity to hero in no time whatsoever. Sprints, dynamic exercises, and hard resistance training with weights increase your testosterone level. Testosterone enables you to build muscle more easily and keeps you lean.

When building muscle, don't do too much endurance exercise. Chronic adherence to the wrong sort of exercise turns you into a wimp. Activities such as long distance running severely hinder muscle building. Exercising like a zero will enable you to run long distances (very slowly), but turn you into a physical wreck. You will feel tired, have no energy and look like a nobody. Exercising like a hero will make you fitter in a much more dynamic and impressive sense. You'll get stronger, develop a killer physique, and feel more confident.

CHALLENGE – For the next ten weeks concentrate only on building muscle and strength. Let everything else take a back seat.

Use these five exercises: squats, rows, bench press, barbell press and barbell curl – if you're not sure how to perform them, look on the internet. Use *only these exercises* twice a week over four gym sessions. Make the weight you use appropriate to the number of repetitions.

Monday

Squats: 6 sets – 8(reps), 5, 5, 5, 5, 8
Bench Press: 6 sets – 10, 8, 5, 5, 4, 10

Tuesday
Barbell Press: 4 sets – 10, 8, 6, 6
Row: 5 sets – 10, 8, 8, 6, 6
Barbell Curl: 4 sets – 10, 8, 8, 5, 12

Thursday
Squats: 5 sets – 10, 6, 4, 4, 15
Bench Press: 5 sets – 8, 6, 4, 4, 3,

Saturday
Barbell Press: 5 sets – 8, 8, 6, 6, 5
Row: 4 sets – 10, 10, 8, 8
Barbell Curl: 5 sets – 10, 10, 8, 8, 5

Have a light warm-up before each exercise then get straight into the work sets. It goes without saying that you're going to have to work hard. These sessions are fairly short so you can give 100% effort and 100% focus. Attack the weights like they're your worst fucking enemy. To enable recovery and adaptation you will need more sleep and 50% more food than you're eating now. Good quality food, protein, carbohydrate and fat. For this five-week period buy some protein powder and make sure you get 50grams of protein straight after training. You will get sore – don't worry, your body will adapt.

After ten weeks you will be far stronger (and you'll realise for yourself how you can alter your body). How much muscle you put on will depend on how hard you've worked, your body type, your individual capacity for muscle growth, if you've eaten enough and if you've had enough sleep.

If you train like this for a year, (with a week off exercise after every five weeks block) your body will be utterly transformed. Your strength will double and you'll look like a superhero. Maybe even your winky will grow.

Claws, Horns, Teeth and Hooves

On Youtube there's a video of four male lions seeking out and attacking a lone male lion, it is brutal. The lion fights heroically for its life but after ten minutes it is so badly injured it can no longer offer resistance. Do the other lions leave it alone? Of course not, even though the lion is longer a threat, they kill it.

You need weapons.

Some time ago I was in a bar in New York talking to a couple ex-special forces guys. They told me about the dozens of guns and thousands of rounds of ammo they had – so they would be prepared for the zombie apocalypse should it happen. The knee jerk reaction to this is think these are guys crazy. But are they? If I was a robber, bandit or jackal with evil intentions I would think twice about targeting their properties. If I did, I'd regret it.

First and foremost, weapons are there to protect yourself; and if *defending yourself* means hurting other people who want to seriously harm you, your loved ones or your family, then so be it. The rule of law protects normal people to a certain extent (because most citizens observe it) but try quoting it to someone who wants to mash-up your face. The lion video is an example of the Law of Nature - the side with the greatest force wins. God help you if you are weak or defenseless, and a crazed lunatic wants to harm you or the people you care about.

Classes of protective 'weapons':

1/ Technological – guns, knives, axes, clubs…i.e. 'arms'
2/ Physical – strength, fighting ability, health
3/ Psychological - confidence, experience, intelligence, adrenal control
4/ Financial – money, assets, land
5/ Legal – national/international law, police, lawyers

Classes 1 and 5 have positives *but* potential problems; the middle three are all positive. Additionally, they can all allow you to take advantage of *opportunities*.

The wider and more developed the classes of weapons you have the more likely you will be able to cope with and survive emergencies of all types; medical emergencies, government crackdowns, street attacks, robberies, business failures, meteor strikes, Godzilla and the Purge. This doesn't mean you can be prepared for everything, that's impossible, there could be situations where only luck determines whether you come out unscathed. Also, just like our heroic lion, you may be overwhelmed by those with more weapons. In which case, go out fighting.

Milo of Croton

Milo of Croton was a legendary 6th Century Greek wrestler famed for his strength. He won many wrestling championships culminating in six Olympic titles. No individual in the modern Olympics has equalled this or even come close. His most famous feat of strength was his ability to carry a four-year-old bull on his shoulders. As a youngster he started carrying a calf around; as the calf matured and grew, Milo matured and grew. The calf grew a little every day and everyday Milo's strength responded to the increased stimulus.

Milo's daily diet allegedly consisted of 9 kilos of meat, 9 kilos of bread, and eighteen pints of wine; even though the wine was watered down, the guy must have been pissed half the time. Even so, the way he built his strength is the cornerstone of strength-training; the blueprint for athletic and sporting success - progressive, incremental steps – gradually increasing the load or stress on the body.

If Milo was alive today he'd be able to crush the normal man - however, his manner of death is interesting and something to be aware of. The story goes that Milo was walking in a forest when he came upon a tree-trunk split with wedges. In what was probably intended as a display of strength, Milo inserted his hands into the cleft to rend (pull apart) the tree. The wedges fell out and the tree closed on his hands, trapping him. Unable to free his hands, the wrestler was killed and eaten by a passing pack of wolves.

No matter his strength and fearsome reputation, Milo was no match for the truly wild.

Whatever your strengths, intelligence, experiences and bravery, there are wild forces in the world which could crush you in an instant, and these forces won't care about it. Don't unnecessarily put yourself in truly dangerous situations, only idiots do that. If you go swimming in a crocodile infested river you are not courageous or brave, you are a moron – and you'll likely be a dead moron. Always be aware of what's going on around you so you can react quickly should anything happen. Most people are walking around with their eyes closed, having no clue of the dangers around them.

Primal and explosively violent forces exist that don't care about anything. Have the sense to be able to recognize them and take appropriate avoidance (or if you can't escape, defence) measures. Milo of Croton's Olympic medals and accolades were no match against a pack of wolves.

Never Been a Better Time to Be a Nobody

There has never been a better time to be a nobody. Some people who are trapped in mental slavery say it is impossible to create something from nothing. Well, what about the Big Bang Theory, the argument that the whole fucking Universe began from an explosion of x from a single tiny point (sounds like bullshit)? Why do 'intelligent' people believe that, yet also believe that a 'nobody' can't escape their background and create a great life? Potential can find a way.

Apparently, racism, prejudice, privilege, class, poor education, social status, parenting and other things work against you and keep you down – that's bullshit, it only does if you believe it and use it as an excuse. Today you have more resources at your command than at any time in the history of humanity. Incredibly, most of these resources are free or minimal cost.

Apps are free, video facilities are free, email is free, websites are pennies, payment processing is free, and ideas are unlimited. Those ideas can be turned into reality; the tools to help you are all around you. The internet means you have the ability to access millions of people. Any interest you have you can find information about it online. Your schooling, educational status and your grade C in English doesn't matter – no one gives a shit about them.

Going from mindless consuming and buying to creating and producing will change your future. The good thing about the enslaved zombies and nerds is they have created tools which you can use to design a new life. The free person should understand that for every free person there necessarily needs to be one-hundred employed people. They have created systems and products which you can use. Thank you, Zombie.

As you build your body and strength, so you can build a better life. Ignore or smash up people who try to stop you or categorise you as some minority victim. Their ideology doesn't help you.

If you want to get on in life you will have to put in the hours, and be prepared to put up with crushing internal and external pressure – you may be so focussed that even not eating won't stop you. You may have to be prepared to look like an 'idiot' whilst others are being sensible and dutifully going to work, paying the bills, and buying useless shit. It doesn't matter, carry on, things will start changing. And when things start changing you will meet other like-minded individuals who will help you rise.

There has never been a better time to be a nobody.

Gang Fit is saying you can rule the world.

- PART TWO -

My old sprint coach once exclaimed, "In every school there's a potential Olympian!" From my experience in coaching, training and being a clever bastard, I think this is indisputable. Every nation that hosts the Olympics talks about how it will boost sport, inclusion, opportunity, health, blah, blah, in their country. It *never* does. It's all part of the pre-Olympic hype. **Gang Fit** is your 'Non-Olympic Legacy', a real fucking legacy, not one made up by committees, experts, overweight ex-Olympians, politicians, social scientists, teachers, government or policy makers.

There's an 'Olympian' in every school; an artist, fighter, criminal, scientist, business builder, explorer, dancer, producer – for every Olympic athlete there are ten thousand Olympian people. Your mission is to create something you can be proud of. Use the street i.e., real life, as your teacher. Whilst you're doing this don't get messed-up by other people's problems. Steer clear of losers, wasters, zombies and people with no energy – they will drain the life-force from you, they're toxic. Life can be like a boulder which you have to push uphill, don't associate with people who make it more difficult. However, once you start succeeding the hill becomes flatter, then it becomes downhill – you pick up momentum. All the while make sure you keep healthy, because health is your supreme asset. If you're ill your life is fucked. Most people don't become ill for no reason; it's the consequence of being a wanker, not caring about their physical condition or what they eat. Your life is fucked anyway because you're going to die; but don't accelerate the damn process! Leave that to the morons who blame their genetics or hormones for their illnesses. Keep strong, build muscle, face physical tests and challenges. But don't just face them, create them; this toughens your body and creates a strong mind. Most people are physically and mentally soft, don't be one of them, they're pathetic - even a tiny wild mouse is tougher than they are.

Gang Fit proposes a different world, a world where a nobody can become a king. Has anyone ever told you that? Your teacher hasn't told you. Your parents haven't told you. Nobody has told you that shit because they don't believe it - which is why they haven't achieved it. Achievement is for *other* people who have special talents, not the likes of you. These people have an illness, and they spread it to other people. You have to murder them in your mind. Leave them behind. The thing is, some of those morons think they're guiding you; doing you a favour by telling you the realities of life. But their realities are bullshit – they are like beetles who've lived all their lives under a stone; eating, shitting, working, sleeping, and breeding. They think this is what makes them knowledgeable – "the realities of life". You shit the same as them, but you don't have to live like them, or listen to their advice gained from living under a stone.

You should create your own legacy – you *can* create your own legacy. Some parents say, "our children are our legacy", true enough, but any moron can have children, it's a product of copulation. Rats have a litter. Pigs have a litter. That makes you no different to a rat or a pig. Children are great but bringing them into this world doesn't make you special. They are necessary for a good life but not sufficient. That's the reality. There are millions of people with kids who are still enslaved, depressed and unfulfilled.

On creating a life, will everything go smoothly? Will you succeed at everything? Fuck, no – get real. But as you progress, many things which once seemed impossible will become eminently possible, until they become nothing at all. They haven't changed, you have changed. Along the way you will meet other people like you. People who are succeeding in life; not because everything is wonderful in their lives, that's impossible, shit happens to everyone, but because they are doing something to create a better life. It doesn't matter your background, colour or education, modern life gives you a zillion opportunities. Most of them you may never come across; it doesn't matter, you'll find, create, or stumble across the ones which are relevant to you. If you are young, whatever your history what you can achieve is mindboggling. All you need to do is smash up your own cowardice, timidity, and fear.

Parts of society moan about poverty, inequality, injustice, discrimination, and scarcity. Ignore all that shit. It does you no good to focus on how terrible life is. How tough life is, is for other people, it shouldn't be your concern. People don't like to hear that message but this is where Gang Fit differs, it contends that the world is improved when the individual improves their life. Focusing on improving your life isn't selfish, it's essential. When your life is improved, the lives of the people who matter to you will also be improved. That will be your Legacy.

Loserville, Somewhere-Town

What is loserville? It's a place where losers live. Where is it? Where you live. How do you get out of it? Don't do what losers do. Then what? Do what losers *don't* do.

Parents are teaching kids to be losers. Schools are teaching kids to be losers. Being a loser is a mindset that is brainwashed into kids at school. Dumb parents who believe they have their kid's best interest at heart go along with it. Unless the child is a natural rebel or has a 'learning disorder' they are groomed into being a clone. Loserville is a virus, a zombie virus; a virus so insidious that people don't know they have it. The point is that society works very well when most of its citizens are losers, it *requires it* - it would fall apart if everyone was free. A society needs 'productive losers' in the way an ant colony needs worker ants. You can fight this by being non-productive (as they see it); not producing what they want but creating what you want. This means you rely on yourself and your band of brothers to create your own world, free from the cancer of the undifferentiated mass. Cancer doesn't view itself as cancer, it's doing what it's meant to do; in the same way that zombies don't realise they are zombies, they are doing what they are programmed to do.

The attraction of Loserville is that some people become very comfortable (even, successful) losers. They have a nice job, a nice house, a nice garden (with herbaceous border), a comfortable life, a good pension and a comfortable death. They've done well. Only an "idiot" would say there's a problem with it. But this is its danger; if there were no upsides no one would do it. Employment, Loserville, Enslavement, Commuting - is an existential crisis not a financial crisis, fucking idiot. It will *never* suit countless millions of people as it makes them feel trapped. No sentient creature on this earth likes being trapped. Animals in zoos develop neuroses because they're trapped. People develop neuroses because of it. *If employment doesn't suit you, you are normal, not abnormal.* You are not the loser, they are. The reason they are isn't financial - it's because they traded freedom, independence and liberty for the security of a monthly wage. Then the fuckers brainwash their children the same way. The kids have got no chance.

A person is not 'winning in life' if they have no self-determination, no matter how much they earn. So, it's always wrong to judge someone by how much money they have without knowing if they are free or not.

Gang Fit doesn't give a shit what other people think, neither should you. When you have no money, losers will tell you why their way of existence is preferable to yours; they'll call *you* a loser. This is because their minds are warped, they can only view things through money, they are hypnotized by it. As far as they are concerned money is the *only* measure. The dumb fucks understand about the idea of starting a business, even though most businesses fail and leave the business owner penniless - yet they can't understand the idea that you are your own business, you are minding your business – you hate being employed because being employed is slavery. You want to be free, not a slave, even if freedom comes with the risk of starving. And when you do well, you succeed, make money and create something amazing, the brain-dead have the nerve to say you did well. How do you think that happened you dumb-fucker slave?

Loserville is a Cancer. It just doesn't know it's a cancer. It's a cancer which is trying to spread. It's an undifferentiated mass. It's your neighborhood. As soon as you step outside of it, you see it.

The Oppressed are the Oppressors

Whatever someone's background, even if you think they are nice - if you're weak they will try to control you. Even the oppressed can become the oppressors. You would think they'd know better, right?

The freed US slaves who were relocated to Liberia in the mid-19th Century, created a cultural and racial caste system in their new home. The Americo-Liberians, as they were called, established plantations and businesses, and became richer than the indigenous people. They began to exercise overwhelming political power, even though they were the minority. They dominated and 'enslaved' the indigenous population. Former slaves created slaves – what sort of bullshit is that? Further, they were religious; they regarded the irreligious indigenous population as little more than animals. Ironic, as many white people in the US thought the former slaves were sub-human - physically and mentally inferior to whites, more like animals.

People who were slaves had become like their former masters. Is there anything more fucked-up?

Never take things for granted, the nicest people may be monsters. The weaker you are the more they will want to dominate you; they just can't help it - they think they are right and you are wrong. History is littered with examples of peoples who were once oppressed becoming the oppressors of other people. It's not that people don't learn, it's that they don't care. Even though they know what it's like to be treated like shit, enslaved, even killed, they are prepared to do it to others.

Get this absolutely straight: Do not be subservient to *anyone*. Do not allow anyone to dominate you. Do not let anyone control you. Do not let anyone tell you how to live your life. It's fine to care about other people and consider what they say. And it's ok to have the normal dynamic of a healthy relationship. But it is not fine to be so dominated by someone that your life is not your own. Once you escape from a relationship like this you realise what a pathetic idiot you've been. Of course, it goes without saying that you owe nothing to the stranger who tries to push you around. It's good to be nice to people, but don't believe you're being nice when you're actually being a weakling. Weaklings eventually get crushed.

It doesn't matter someone's history; whether they've been tormented, abused, enslaved or treated like shit. If you are weak, they will do start doing the same to you; and you'll deserve it.

Donuts Can Make You Fit

<u>CHALLENGE</u> - Find a 5-storey plus, building. In the city that's pretty easy to do. You can use the stairs for a superb workout. However, some blocks have a security guard. If so, the first time you go, bung them a fiver and ask if you can use the stairs for a workout. After that take them a donut every time you visit. Security people love donuts because most are out-of-shape, bored-out-of-their-mind people who are out-of-options. Giving them a donut will make their day. Eventually they'll look forward to your visit. They might even invite you back to their place to meet the wife and disabled kid.

[Note: Everything can be used for something other than its primary intention. In this instance a donut becomes a bribe. A paper clip can become a weapon, and beer can be used to trap slugs. Used in a different way, a photo of a bear may be more dangerous than a real bear]

You may live in a block of flats, or know some stairs which are not in a building – you can use those. It will save you the donut money. But you'll miss out on meeting nazi-in-a-uniform. Ok, ok, security guards aren't all Nazis, but Gang Fit has to be consistent.

<u>Session</u>: Walk up the stairs and back down five times. Do this twice a week.

Progression:

1 Once walking is easy – walk faster. Once that is easy, run up the stairs. Eventually you'll be able to sprint up the stairs. How you achieve that is up to you. The aim is to be able to sprint up the stairs five times in a row. You always *walk* back down for recovery. Before you can sprint all five in a row you may need to do one lot fast, the next normal, and so on.

2 When you can sprint up the stairs, get some 20lb dumbbells (or kettlebells) with good grips. Go back to walking up the stairs holding them in each hand. When you do this go up as flat-footed as you can. Naturally, you will come down on your toes.

3 Once you can do this you should do one session, sprint up the stairs, and one session, walk up with weights, per week.

This is a *significant* workout for your legs, heart and lungs. You may feel light-headed when you first start, but persist, it won't last. The lower limbs and cardio-respiratory system are your power generators. Developing these turns you into an unstoppable beast.

Ever see those films where some sort of disaster or crises happens? Who are the first to die? The old, the unfit, the obese, the stupid and the unlucky. There's nothing you can do about bad luck, shit happens – but being fit, robust and dynamic can only be good; it is an insurance policy for when unholy bullshit strikes:

- It gives you a greater ability to avoid, escape. or deal with sudden street-level life-threatening events – you come out unscathed or less harmed than others. You live to fight another day. Being healthy and strong enhances your ability to cope with the variations and challenges of life. Life is a stress test; random events are stress tests. Banks are subject to stress tests to see if they can cope with fluctuations, outliers and extreme situation. Your assets to survive real-life stress tests are physical strength and robust health. Jesus, some people keel-over from having to run for the bus; they need oxygen to recover. It's their only exercise for a month. They deserve it, lazy fucks.

- The disaster that everyone faces is getting old. People have insurance policies for all sorts of things, their cars, their houses, inability to work, and so on - but the average person doesn't look after their health, even though they *know* aging is going to happen. Some young people think they are healthy, when, in fact, their health is mostly a function of youth not because they look after themselves. They eventually learn their lesson. As they age, they start suffering from the same conditions that older people suffer from. So, it's not only about being able to cope with the short-term risks of meteor-strikes, being chased by zombies or novel viruses, but the long-term risk that everyone faces. The way to see the long-term risk is to look at people older than yourself. What do they look like? What are they suffering from? Those fossils are a window into your future if you don't look after your health.

****

View stair training as an insurance policy, money in the health bank, an anti-aging strategy. However, unlike all the other insurance policies it pays out benefits every day, in that you feel unstoppable. You'll live forever. Buy some donuts and get to it.

True Natural Rebel

The vast majority of kids who were rebels at school end up enslaved as adults. They were never true rebels. The true natural rebel is very often a quiet unassuming school-kid, not the violent uncontrollable one who ends up broken like a wild horse. Real rebels don't look like rebels. You can look like anything you want but don't believe that *just* because you look different you *are* different. Many young people desperately try to look different; this in itself is a sign of conformity. Looking different ain't shit. Buying fancy clothes or dying your hair purple isn't non-conformity, any fool can do that, it takes no effort.

Teachers teach you useless shit to become employable. You need to drop that nonsense and become unemployable. A rebel doesn't care what other people know because no matter what people know, they are still trapped. When you're a rebel people will regard you as brainless, an idiot; "When are you going to grow up?" "Why don't you get a job?" "Why can't you be more like your sister?" If you don't care what they say, it will irritate them, but that's fine, they don't own you.

****

Being a drop-out and not doing shit won't get you anywhere. That's being a rebel without a brain. Plenty of kids don't conform but they are just lazy lard-arses, watching Netflix, playing video games, and eating junk food all day. If you are unemployed you should be *gainfully* unemployed. If you are employed (why?), you should be *gainfully employed in your non-work time*. This is the only way you will escape normal society. It's fine to have fun and enjoy life, but whilst you're doing it, you should be learning something. Employment tells you that you should you work at the office/shop/factory and have leisure at home. Do the opposite, waste as little mental energy at work as you can get away with, and work towards something outside. The same with school. If a teacher asks; "Johnny! Why are you slacking?" Tell them you've enrolled into the 'School of Gang Fit'.

The School of Gang Fit is one where you find out stuff for yourself; it is not spoon-fed to you by a teacher. You decide your own subjects, not them. Where you learn more from *doing the test* than you do from revising for the test. At school the lesson comes before the test, this is arse about tits – the opposite to real life.
Being a true rebel requires a brain even though people will say it's brainless. Essentially, it's not even being a rebel! It's being real and forging your own life. To normal people, looking after yourself and not giving a damn about what they are concerned about makes you an outsider. It is an act of defiance - you are a rebel in their eyes. A real rebel is not a rebel for the sake of it; they are just someone who is creating their own life, free of the concerns of others. That makes them dangerous.

This is important - it needs repeating. *You need to be in control of your life*. This one thing will make you diverge from your loser friends.

Kids who don't care about the consequences of their actions are uncontrollable. Society doesn't know what to do with them. The problem is that most of them aren't doing anything to control their own lives – they eat junk food, play video games into the early morning and talk stupid shit to each other. If you are "out-of-control" in the normal world, you *have to be in control* of your world. Being an idiot in both worlds won't get you anywhere, you'll end up broke or in prison. A total loser. An uber loser. A total, uber loser. Worse even than the employed losers. Don't give a shit about the normal ways of society or what they think, *but do give a shit how you think and what you do*. Be a rebel with a brain.

Avoid Sea Monsters

A long time ago, when big ships were made from giant Oaks, some sailors spied an island in the middle of the ocean - so they set towards it. They had spent weeks at sea and were desperate to be on dry land. As they sailed closer they observed that the island had no trees and was featureless. Anyway, on arrival they dropped anchor and alighted on the island. To celebrate their good fortune they took food and beer with them so they could have a feast. They lit a fire to cook whatever it was that sailors used to eat when ships were made from wood. However, after a couple of minutes the 'island' began to lurch and shake violently, heaving up and down and side to side. Finally, it rose into the air then plunged down beneath the waves, taking the sailors with it, and smashing their ship into a million pieces. The sailors had unwittingly settled upon the back of a massive sleeping sea monster which had woken after they lit the fire.

There is some good news. The salty sea-dogs had the most honourable death – death at sea. They died with their boots on.

****

Some things may look like a fine idea, but they're not. If our sailors had been a bit more observant they would have realised there was something not right about the island - but in their desire to get onto dry land they were careless.

The good thing about being young is you have enough time to come back from mistakes, but some mistakes are so dumb you may never recover – stupid shit like trying to kiss a shark, stroke a hyena, or betting your life on Arsenal winning the Premiership. In your mission to escape slow death by zombiefication, it's good to try random *non-life-threatening* stuff. It opens the door to opportunity and hidden chance. The fancy way I've heard it said is, *"life should be a portfolio of safe-to-fail experiments"*. Try out different stuff; no one can see with absolute certainty where success will come from.

Avoid crap which is life and health threatening. Don't put yourself in the position where you can lose lots of money. I know someone who guaranteed the debts of a business for a friend, using his house as security. He also gave the business a few thousand to help start, with no guarantee of return. What do you think happened? Let's just say, they are no longer friends. Life teaches lessons you don't get at school.

As our sailors found out, some dangers are hidden. Clued-up people can smell them though, they know the dangers. Be clever and not an idiot. Don't be taken in by people trying to sell you a monster. Sometimes it may be a friend selling you a monster, a dumb idea which has the potential to harm you. Don't be nervous or guilty about turning them down. Saying no to a friend is far better than falling out when the shit turns sour. Friends' falling out because of a failed venture is very common.

Note: Some things may look like 'monsters' but they're not – it's just your fear or lack of confidence stopping you. So, you need to distinguish between the real monsters and the monsters inside your head.

Expendable in Emergencies

It's said that the first role of a government is to protect its citizens – this isn't true, as the first role of government is to *protect itself,* then to protect others.

This is the hierarchy of governmental priorities:

1 Protect itself
2 Protect 'society'
3 Protect citizens
4 Protect you
5 Protect criminals
6 Protect animals

There are greater priorities than protecting you. You are fourth on the list, just above criminals. This means you are expendable in emergencies for the protection of the categories above you. There are situations where your government would actively harm you, or knowingly allow you to be harmed for the 'greater good'.

We've all seen the films where some sort of virus, which turns people murderously insane, hits a town, part of the city, or some remote place. What happens when the authorities get wind of what's happening? They put the entire place on lock-down; no one can leave or enter. An attempt to stop the virus from spreading. This is an understandable and necessary strategy - but woe betide those who are trapped in the infected area, they become collateral damage. Sacrificed for the sake of others. You cannot blame the authorities for doing that, it's their duty.

Here's the thing: Sometimes circumstances will dictate that you will be harmed or come out the worse, and no one will be to blame, it's not personal. In a sinking ship would a parent save their child or you? You think you have been treated unfairly? With this is mind we can clear up some claptrap. People are too busy being victims, complaining why life is so uniquely hard for them. Don't be like that. Some things will turn out shit and no one will be to blame; not your parents, friends, partner or the government – it's just circumstance. Life doesn't hate you. Life is indifferent. It doesn't know you exist. You are nothing. You could be extinguished instantly for no particular reason, and hardly anyone in the world would give a damn. It's nothing personal. There's a video on YouTube of a Stork deliberately throwing one of her chicks out of the nest to enhance the survival probability (due to the supply of food) of her other chicks – rather two healthy chicks than three underfed. Talk about a bad day for that chick, mothers are meant to protect their offspring, right?

Example 1: I lived in a small village in the country for three years. Being very flat, and at sea level, the whole region was prone to flooding. Over the years, pumping stations, drains and sluices had been built to protect the area from flooding. However, one particular year the flooding was so severe that people were trapped in their villages with no way out other than by boat. The roads had become rivers. To protect the areas with the most houses and inhabitants, the flood water was deliberately drained and pumped into the less populated areas. The smaller villages were overwhelmed. Many farms were under feet of water for weeks. The authorities had decided this was the only way to reduce the overall damage. Save the bigger areas, flood the smaller areas.

Example 2: Power black-outs happen every now and then, right? Most people have experienced them. Maybe a power line is down, demand for electricity has outstripped supply, or a generator is down. A national power grid has spare capacity for when things go wrong. What happens when things go more wrong? In the UK a while back, the trains (in a large area of the country) stopped running. The electricity supply to the signaling facilities of the rail network was cut off – this meant the trains had to stop. Even though the supply was only cut off for only ten minutes, the trains were fucked for hours.

71

Most people, because they are morons, have no idea why this happened; all they were concerned about was that it disrupted their commute home from work. When everything returned to normal they went back to brain-dead slavery mode. Me, being free-like-a-bird and having my own time, wanted to know what happened. After a bit of digging about I found this explanation from an electricity system expert. Here's his summary:

'A frequency trace to which we have access at Strathclyde shows that the fall in system frequency was arrested by the combination of responses on the system but dropped to below 49.2 Hz. However, the trace also shows a second drop in frequency about a minute after the first one. With much of the scheduled frequency response capacity having been exhausted and not yet replaced, system frequency subsequently fell to less to 48.8 Hz at which point the first stage of **'Low Frequency Demand Disconnection'** **(LFDD) operated.** LFDD is an 'automatic defence measure' installed on the distribution networks and designed to save the system from a complete collapse. It does so through restoring the balance between generation and demand by opening **circuit breakers** on portions of the distribution network to disconnect demand. It works in 9 successive tranches, each triggered if system frequency continues to fall.'

'The first tranche of LFDD, the only one that was triggered on Friday, is intended to disconnect 5% of demand under **Operating Code No. 6 (OC6)**. However, on Friday, the disconnected demand seemed to include supplies to Network Rail signalling facilities. This, in turn, caused interruptions to train services. Even though system frequency was restored to around 50 Hz within 10 minutes of the initial generation losses (partly as a result of the demand disconnection) and National Grid said that "By 6.30pm, all demand was restored by the distribution network operators", restoration of rail services took much longer.'

Note the parts in bold - the power grid acted in the same way as the flood defence system in the earlier example, it harmed one area to defend the whole system. However, the process was automatic, no human decision making was involved in triggering the defence mechanism. Further, something went wrong, the shutting down of the signaling supply was an unintentional consequence – a mistake.

As we descend deeper into a Skynet Society, when the shit hits the fan, no humans will be involved, no emotions, and no conscience – your fate will be decided by an automated procedure. If that's not bad enough, it may fuck up. Nothing personal.

Example 3: People are under the illusion they own their land or property if they have no mortgage or debt on it. This is never true, the Government can take it from anyone at any time, and for any bullshit reason they make up. In the 1940's the UK government took over an *entire village* and never gave it back – they turned it into a Ministry of Defence war games area. The government said they'd give it back, but they didn't. In

China, whole valleys with hundreds of villages have been flooded to make giant dams for electricity generation. Hundreds of thousands of citizens forced to leave everything they know. In this case, protecting (benefiting) society comes before protecting citizens.

Compulsory Purchase, Eminent Domain, or Land Acquisition, depending what country you're in, means the State has the power to seize or demolish your property (or land) for the 'public good', or some sort of grand project; a hyper-speed rail line, Olympic development, airport runway, a vanity project, and so on. They can also seize where you have your business. Ok, they are meant to compensate the owner, or offer a suitable place for relocation, but the point is there is no choice. They decide, and you are the collateral damage. The Government can steal your family home even if you've done nothing wrong. Additionally, compulsory purchase orders can be used to acquire land which *benefits a private interest* - homes in Islington, London, were purchased (stolen) to build the Emirates Stadium for Arsenal Football Club. You don't own shit.

****

Cloud Cuckoo Land is thinking the Government will always look after your best interests. You are not their first interest. You are not even their second or third interest. You are just above the criminal in the list of their priorities. In the scenario of zombie attacks, virulent spreading viruses or alien invasions, the poor or affected areas will be jettisoned for the greater good. This won't be considered a crime because the situation will have necessitated it.

Gang Fit proposes that you can reverse this. The government, society, and its citizens shouldn't be your priorities. You should be your number one priority. In an emergency situation all those knobs are expendable if necessary, for your survival. Nothing personal. If you do this it will probably be viewed as a crime – yet you would only be doing what the State would do in an emergency. It is entirely ethical to put yourself (and your family, or whoever you care about) first. It would be ethically wrong not to. What would happen if others were eliminated for your greater good? Easy, you'd be put in prison. But in an extreme situation, society would break down, the police and army would have other priorities, the phones wouldn't work, and there'd be no public transport. There would be no system to arrest you or put you in prison. Normal life would cease. The jackals would come out and you'd have to take matters into your own hands.

In your own life, the people and things which don't mean much to you are expendable. You've no doubt thought what you would do if you were on a sinking ship or some sort of disaster situation, yet normal life is a long-term disaster if you don't focus on the things that matter. Life is a slow train wreck if you let it get out of your control. Jettison the people who contribute to your hardship – *it is your moral duty*. There are only two or three things in life which are <u>very important,</u> and one-hundred things which are of medium importance. The medium important things will never make up for the very important things. In an emergency you should view all the things below 'very important' as expendable, because in an emergency *you* will be expendable.

****

When civilized society collapses, it will do so in an instant. You go to bed safe and secure; when you wake up, everything has changed - your old life will be dead. There was a storm in the UK a while back. Gusts of wind reached 60mph in London – this stopped 80% of the trains running. A bit of fucking wind! When some real shit happens, everything will stop, nothing will run. The gas stations will run out of fuel. Phones won't work and power generation will stop. You won't have access to cash, which won't matter as the shops won't be open – people will loot them to get food and water. You won't be able to get in touch with the people you care about.

TASK – This is straightforward and can be implemented now. Choose an address where all the people you care about should meet in the case of a real crisis; your family, loved ones, pet llama, whatever. Everyone should try to get there any way they can, from wherever they are, however long it takes, two hours to two weeks. Everyone will wait at that address until the last person has arrived. This means that the most important people in your life are all together. From there you can decide what to do as a group. It is not for anyone to think, be clever, or second-guess – *just get to that address*. It needs to be an automatic response to some sort of societal collapse when all communications have been cut. Is this paranoid? Yes. Paranoia means survival, as long as it doesn't make you run from one threat into the jaws of a larger threat.

Ultimately, you (and your loved ones) are expendable. It's nothing personal. You need to turn that around. In emergencies protect yourself and your clan before anything else. Other people as collateral damage. It's not nice, but survival is primal, it is wild - it is the evolutionary history of the planet.

Never Had a CV

What's a CV? It's the acronym for Curriculum Vitae, which means, '*I need a job*', in Latin.
When I left school I was pretty clueless. I hadn't been taught there were ways to live other than being a full-time employee. I'd been brainwashed into conformity. I put on my only suit and went to an employment agency who told me I needed a CV to help me get a job. I had no idea what a CV was, and I didn't know Latin because I went to

a modern school where it was regarded as an unnecessary, dead language. [Note: *All the top private schools teach Latin, so they must know something that shit schools don't. If you're a normal street kid in a gang, and you teach yourself Latin, it will confuse the hell out of the people you meet – they won't be able to bracket you. This one thing can help alter your life, not necessarily because you can read Latin shit, but that any preconceived notions that people have about you will change*].

As I was just out of school my CV only contained my school history, exam results, hobbies and interests – eleven years of schooling reduced to this. The employment agency also gave me a twenty-minute maths and english test which was so easy I completed it in seven seconds. So, now I was registered with the agency. It worked because I got an interview at a bank within a week. Unfortunately, the interview went well and they employed me.

For about a year I was happy, I had money in my pocket, and I worked in the centre of an exciting City. But it didn't last. A sense of unease started to creep in, the novelty was wearing off - I began to feel trapped. I remember looking at the older employees at the bank; they looked unhealthy and half-dead, devoid of vitality. This wasn't what I wanted. I quit.

****

I hadn't yet figured out that it wasn't the bank which was the problem, *but employment itself*. After the bank, the jobs I had were sales related. Sales jobs don't give a shit about your exams, qualifications, or that you do macramé in your spare time – all they care about is that you can sell. They filter out the hopeless applicants in the interview (or during the phone call for the interview); the people who pass normally have a period, say, of two weeks where they are thrown into the deep end, sink or swim. If they can't sell, they're out. I remember having an interview on the 33rd floor of a building in Canary Wharf (the centre of finance and fraud, in London) – no CV was asked for. I passed, of course. On the first day I noticed the mix of salespeople, it was completely diverse. The employer didn't care who we were, what age, what colour, what gender or how we dressed. It was still a bullshit job though, because most jobs are bullshit - but a CV didn't mean anything to them. Note: They regarded degrees the same way. A degree doesn't mean diddly-squat when it comes to selling. They ran an evolutionary system, survive or die. The most effective system there is.

I promised myself to never again have a CV. Further, I realised that the jobs which required a CV were *precisely* the type of job I didn't want. Any jobs that needed a CV, I filtered out. A CV is like, "I've been a good boy, been employed, done all sorts of amazing work-related things, and was a key member of the sales force (*as if*). I like travel, reading and socialising with friends. Once I cycled from London to Paris and

75

raised £2k for my local hospice*". Translated: *"Please hire me, please hire me, I'm desperate. I hate my job, the pay is shit and I'm going nowhere."*

Ok, so I lied, I did have a CV but only for a year or two until I came to my senses. The CV experts tell you how a CV should be presented, and that it shouldn't show long periods of unemployment – well, that's people like me fucked; I spent half my life gainfully unemployed, a CV would be pure fiction. The thing is, most employed people lie on their CV; this is called 'tailoring it to the job you're applying for'.

****

What do you want? You can have a 'CV Life' or a 'Non-CV Life'. The majority choose the former because they don't know any better. When you're employed in the type of shit job which requires a CV, you are surrounded by other people like you. You socialise with them. Youu marry one of them. Then you have kids. Then you brainwash your kids into the same world. A self-perpetuating loop of zombiefication. A living hell of slavery where slaves give birth to and raise other slaves. There are definitely people around who are happy with slavery, it makes them feel secure; they are born with the slavery gene. There are others whose environment creates it in the way a long-term prisoner becomes institutionalised. So, it's possible the slavery mindset is one part nature, one part nurture. If you have a 'predisposition for enslavement' and you are surrounded by that mindset as you grow-up, you become willing fodder for the slave nation. We have to ask ourselves, is the zombie happy being a zombie? They may well be. They go to zombie pubs, watch zombie sports, form zombie institutions and talk zombie-talk.

If you are happy living in Zombie-World, be my guest. Work all your life, retire, then die. All of it will be summarised in your CV which your relatives can keep on their mantelpiece, next to the urn of your ashes

Starving in a Sea of Plenty

For two years my daughter and I had a set of keys to the pier of a popular resort on the English coast. How it came about that two townies were given the authority to open an entire pier for their own use is still a mystery to me. This meant that after the pier had closed we could let ourselves in and do some fishing with no holiday makers, boats, or scuba divers (the arch enemy) getting on our tits.

Question: *Why is it that two people can fish off practically the same spot of a pier but their catch is wildly different?*

Two examples, learned from experience:

1/ We were getting hacked-off. An hour or so after the pier closed the fish would stop biting. Particularly annoying, as we were looking forward to a few hours fishing free from the presence of day-trippers. One evening, when buying some knackered looking ragworm from the angling shop, the owner advised us that after a certain time we should present the bait lower down - this would enable us to catch the bottom-feeders. Later that night, we did just that; a depth adjustment to a sliding rig of around ten feet, attracted bites almost immediately. When we first tried this it was like a miracle. The scaly fuckers had been within reach all the time - literally a few feet away but we hadn't realised.

First lesson: A simple depth adjustment of the bait opened up a whole new world of fish.

Sea-life is split into marine layers (amongst other things) like the rock strata on the face of a cliff. Bottom-feeders tend to stay on the bottom; they rarely go near the surface to feed. Mid-water and surface feeders do the same thing.

2/ When we first starting sea-fishing seriously we bought some nice big fancy floats which we thought would do the job. We wanted bigger floats as smaller ones were harder to see in the sea swell. For the first few days there were plenty of fish testing the bait but very few definite bites. We knew there were fish around due to the amount of 'knocks' on the floats. One day an experienced fisherman passed by, so we spoke to him about our frustration. He knew what the problem was. He advised us to use smaller floats; "the problem is your floats are too big, when the fish try the bait they feel the resistance of the float, so they spit it out". Stupid us, we were using floats big enough to be seen easily in the sea but *hadn't thought it might not suit the fish.* They sensed there was something wrong as soon as they felt an unaccustomed resistance due to the buoyancy of the float. When we swapped to smaller floats we started hooking the fish.

Second lesson: We only thought about our point of view, not the p.o.v. of the fish.

****

The more knowledge an angler has the more fish they catch relative to the inexperienced. The newbie may catch hardly anything and when asked why, responds, "there are no fish around" or, "they're not biting". An inexperienced angler could fish all day in an area alive with fish but come away with zilch.

The Kalahari bushmen, indigenous aboriginals and other hunter-gatherer dudes know that to effectively track, trap, or catch an animal you have to *become that animal*; see the world through its eyes. So it is with fishing, the more experienced you become the more you understand the mind of the fish you are trying to catch.

My daughter and I have enough experience that we can generally tell the type of fish (before seeing it) simply from the way it takes the bait, and the signature pull on the line. We also appreciate that fish have an undeserved reputation; every angler knows that fish aren't the dumb 'five-second memory' creatures that people think they are - yes, they are creatures of habit, but so are humans.

****

You understand all this shit about fishing is a metaphor, right?

<u>Money and opportunity is everywhere, all the time.</u>

The saying goes that, 'God hides opportunity by hiding it next to you'. Gang fit doesn't give a fuck about God, but opportunity *is* everywhere. If you think it is, it is. If you think it isn't, it isn't. Your parents, teachers, and other adults may have damaged your brain with the scarcity mindset, "there's not enough to go round!" This is complete bollocks, there is so much opportunity it is oozing from every crack in the pavement. Just adjust your mindset like we adjusted our bait. Don't be like the inexperienced fisherman who catches nothing in a sea of plenty.

Run for the Bus

Someone said, "never run for a bus", meaning you should determine how you live, and not be at the mercy of circumstance. I get it, but add another view, "*run for the bus, because you can, even though it's not necessary*". Isn't that why people climb mountains? In a way, it *is* necessary, very necessary - you do it *precisely* because you can - so it needs doing.

Your mind wants comfort, it will come up with all sorts of reasons why you shouldn't exert yourself; this is an evolutionary survival mechanism – to get food for the least amount of effort. A long time ago, the natural environment didn't care what you wanted; you needed to earn your food. All you need to do now is catch the number 22 bus to the supermarket. As you no longer live in the wild, you have to recreate it by making your life more physically challenging.

No living creature in the history of the world has had a default setting of physical comfort. Too much comfort is an early grave. Comfort has its place, but modern life is making it too easy to be a lazy, overweight loser. "Oh, it's my genes!" No, it's the cake. Plus the only exercise you get is going to the fridge to get it.

Think of running for the bus as earning your calories. Think of physical work as hunting for your food. Think of cycling fifty miles as tracking an antelope. Climbing trees, jumping over walls, running up-stairs, fighting, throwing, sprinting – they're reproducing things your ancient ancestors had to do to survive Again; you have to *expend calories to get calories* because the modern environment no longer forces you do it. The closest to a wild environment is being in a Street Gang, with its periods of inaction and intense action, adrenaline, and psychological danger. This is because young people are still wild. Yet people say that is wrong. Society doesn't like wildness. It's scared by it. It will try to stop you from being wild. It wants you to conform, but as soon as you conform your life-force and spirit is dead.

Make your normal life physically harder. *Purposely* create physical challenges. Run for the bus, run across the road, jump walls; whatever – you do it because you can. You do it because you are recreating a wild environment. You do it because the fossils around you can't, and you don't want to be like them.

National Slipper Index

Do you live in a part of the City where women (and old men) go to the local shops in their slippers? What's the area like? I'm not talking about student areas or university towns but areas where usual people live.

There's an ex-fishing town (now a wasteland) on the east coast of England. The women go to the shops in their *pyjamas*. What's that about? Can't they afford clothes? There seems to be variations of this in every country - apart from Norway, which is fucking perfect. We need a National Slipper Index. There are apps you can use when you're looking to move to a different area - they provide local information such as pollution, crime levels, amount of green spaces, types of schools, and so on; why not an app which gives stats on how many locals do their shopping in slippers? It would tell you everything you need to know about an area. You can take avoidance measures. But if you *had* to go into an area of many slippers, you can make sure you are prepared for any problems which may arise. A mask to filter out the cigarette and dope smoke. Anti-zombie spray. Samurai sword. Different currencies for the local shop. A language translation app set to 'local inbred'. A mirror so you don't need to look directly at anyone's face. An extra pair of lungs. Glucose tablets and an EpiPen.

If you live in an area with a high slipper rating, your aim should be to move. It is better to live in 'shit-house in nice-area' than 'nice-house in shit-area'; this is because you can improve your house, but you can't improve your area. If you live in shit-area, shit will *always* come to your door.

There is nothing intrinsically bad about slippers. But they should be worn inside not outside. Slippers are good in the right environment but evil in the wrong environment. You think this is a joke? It isn't. High slipper areas are associated with more crime, more violence, more pollution, more heart disease, more lung disease, worse shops and more junk food outlets. Get out.

Stop Being Nice

TEST – There are times to be nice, and times not to rock the boat for the sake of harmony. That's understandable. You don't want disagreements all the time. Live and let live, and all that. Now, for the next six months, every time someone talks shit you don't agree with – tell them in no uncertain terms that you don't agree. Don't let it ride for the sake of 'niceness'. After all, they are bending your ears back with their views, did you ask for that? It's rude.

What are the benefits of this?

Firstly, it stops people talking crap to you and taking you for granted. They learn not to spew verbal diarrhea in your direction. *Secondly*, if you don't actively disagree with them they may believe you *actually agree with them*, it reinforces their delusions. So you'll be doing them a favour. *Thirdly*, it teaches you how to deal with confrontation and uncomfortable situations. Many people are nice, not because they *are* nice, but that they're scared of making a scene so they end up listening to endless drivel from idiots. That's not good; it harms you, wastes your time, and offends your dead ancestors who fought against fascism. *Fourth(ly)*, once you get used to this, it's fun; in fact it's hilarious. Watch their reactions. You are doing something they hardly ever come across in polite society. They can't handle it.

Gluten Free

A while back I bumped into an old friend I hadn't seen for years. She was pushing a pale-looking ginger kid in a pram. After the usual stuff people say when they meet someone they haven't seen for a long time, she got talking about the diet of her two-year old son [When most people have young kids they can't stop talking about them, they don't realize that people with no kids find that more boring than watching paint dry]. "I think Timmy is gluten intolerant so I don't give him normal biscuits, I have to buy him gluten-free biscuits. But they are three times more expensive than normal biscuits!" Being contrary, I asked her why she was wasting her money. "Why are you buying gluten-free biscuits? He doesn't need *any* biscuits". Of course, she couldn't process this in her post-birth shrunken brain. She looked at me as if I had said, "your child comes from Venus". What I said was *preposterous* to her. What sort of monster wouldn't give their child biscuits? This made me a Nazi.

The truth is *always* preposterous to people who are stuck in zombie world. They have lived one life, it's impossible for them to accept that the fundamental realities of how they live and what believe, is just a construct.

Life shouldn't be gluten-free, it should be free of the things which contain gluten, not those fucking things with the gluten taken out. Gluten is the name for a group of proteins found in cereal grains - just stop eating cereals, you don't need them! They're non-essential. In the same way, you should drop the shit from your life, not replace it with a lesser version of shit. Even in small quantities, shit smells like shit. If you hate employment, earning more money won't make it better. Money if you're in a prison is pretty useless. Maybe you can burn it to keep warm or wipe your arse if you run out of bog roll.

If you have read the first Gang Fit you know that the fastest way to improve your life is to get rid of all the stuff you hate. Get rid of it! It doesn't matter if other people don't mind it (or like it), *if you hate it*, that's all that matters. Even if you are the only person on earth who hates it.

Don't be stuck in Timmy's mum's world. The idea of not giving her son biscuits was so ridiculous to her, that she paid three times as much to buy gluten free ones. This is how far humanity has come – from hunter-gatherers who caught and slaughtered wild animals, drank their blood, and lived under the stars - to weak, brain-dead individuals who give their dopey looking kids gluten-free biscuits.

It's more important to be idiot free than gluten free. Whatever is not good for you, *don't accept any of it*. No person, teacher, institution or government has the authority to tell you otherwise.

Circuit Training

What's good about circuit training:

1 Anyone can do it
2 You don't need a gym
3 Equipment isn't necessary
4 It costs nothing
5 It can varied in a zillion ways
7 You can make it easy or brutally hard

What's bad about circuit training:

1 Nothing

Circuits are old-skool, and new-skool. They're like an exercise version of a bicycle – something which is old but also something of the present and future. Circuit training has lasted the test of time.

For the non-athlete wanting to get fit, circuit training is the bomb. Doing a circuit once a week is a quick and compact way of working out. Any type of exercise can be included, it's only limited by your imagination. Circuits can be varied according to your desired outcome; focusing on heart rate, endurance, strength endurance, lactic tolerance, whatever. You can use weights, medicine balls, resistance bands, any equipment you like - or just body weight. Body parts can be specifically targeted; I've done circuits using only six different waist exercises, an absolute killer; for a week, every time I coughed my waist hurt. It was great. You can add in sprints, shadow boxing, anything you like.

Here's a suggestion:

1st Set

Push-Ups x 20
Tuck Jumps x 10
Chinnies x 20
Mountain climbs x 36

2nd Set

Bench Dips x 40
Barbell curls x 10
Burpees x 10
Waist (variations) x 20

3rd Set

Barbell Shoulder Press x 10
Split Jumps x 24
Side Raises x 20 (each side)
Push-Ups x 20
Chinnies x 20

[Each set is performed three times over with a few seconds between each exercise. The rest interval between sets is five minutes]

In your mission to get fitter, stronger, and dynamically robust, it is a mistake to *only* to concentrate on a few gym exercises such as squats, deadlifts, and shoulder press. Whilst they are excellent exercises for strength, they are not enough for systemic health. In fact, if you lived in China and the government declared, "you can only do *one* type of exercise twice a week, or you'll be tortured, cooked, and eaten" – you should choose circuits over the 'big three' gym exercises. It would better for your overall health. Don't be a meathead.

Note: If you're not sure what these exercises are, you have the Internet FFS – look them up! People have access to 90% of the world's information online, yet they still ask dumb questions.

Coping Strategies

Living in a shithole part of London I realised I'd been using coping strategies to get by. The effect of these strategies was to block-out or neutralise the crap around me by *injecting life with beauty.* Why do I use the word 'beauty' in a book called Gang Fit? Because if you have no beauty in life, it's not worth living. Existing in a grey ugly world eventually turns a person into a dead being, deprived of magic. You should be inheriting the world and creating something fucking amazing – that's beautiful.

Although life is improved more by removing the shit rather than spraying it with perfume (i.e., leaving a job you hate rather than alleviating it by earning more) sometimes, temporarily, you may have no choice – you get stuck in a rut for a while.

Whilst walking through shit town I'd decide to only take notice of the flowers and trees – touching them, smelling them, seeing the type of insects they attracted. I must have looked like a weirdo. I challenged myself to identify the trees from looking only at their outline, the bark, or by the shape of their leaves. With my eyes closed I taught myself to identify the birch, oak, ash and willow just from the *smell* of their leaves. This had a completely immersive effect, blocking out the grime, rubbish and bullshit around me. On social media I'd post photos of the different types of leaves I'd picked; and the nuts and fruit which Nature (even in shit town) had supplied.

Use whatever coping strategies you need. Look forwards to a better reality. Have a goal, objective, or some type of dedication you can be absorbed in. This is not denying reality but transporting yourself to a better world – a world you will one day create. A coping strategy does two things; it blocks out any shit you may be surrounded by (a force field); and it allows you to concentrate on your plans without anything dragging you down.

Kid Conquers World

I knew a kid who conquered the world.

I first met him at a theatre in a boring provincial town. He was one of the ensemble dancers in a Christmas pantomime. He loved dance; that was his world. He did poorly at school, he wasn't academic. His real dad wasn't around. His mum had taken him to the local dance school at an early age.

One day I read a report in the local newspaper that he had appeared at the local magistrates' court. An argument with his step-father had turned physical. I don't know what the outcome of the court appearance was - however, this is what finally gave him the motivation to escape from the cage of his background and the nothingness of 'boring town' - a place where the only aspiration was to have a fish, chips and mushy peas on a Friday night. A place where a treat was to have a two-course meal at the out-of-town supermarket cafeteria. *So he escaped.* He hardly had any money, but he moved to the Big City. This is where a dancer should be - there was no point being the best dancer in a small town. He stayed with friends in a small flat. He went to dance studios for classes. He met other dancers. He signed up with a city agency. Every spare moment he was dancing. He posted his own dance videos (which he choreographed) on social media. Because he was talented, dedicated and hard-working, an agent soon got him jobs as a commercial dancer. When he wasn't working and earning good money, he was busy connecting with other dancers, producing dynamic and original dance videos. He didn't stop. He was creating a new life. Every now and then he would go back to Boring Town to see old friends and family – it was like a different world, it had nothing for him. When someone *escapes* their background, they may revisit for a while, but eventually they never return – it is dead to them.

As time went on, the work he got was better paid; he got jobs abroad – eventually, he got a position in a show which toured the world. Even then he was still posting his own dance videos from the places he was at, China, the US, Spain. When the show's tour came to an end he moved to New York, he met more dancers, did more videos and got more work. Agents saw his videos on social media, they went to him, he didn't need to go to them. He started getting jobs with globally known singers, dancing in their videos, and next to them on stage. He was travelling the world, earning a load of money and having the time of his life.

****

The point of this is that he didn't stop. He went from a normal background, doing Christmas performances at Boring Town dance school (where it all started), to travelling the world doing the stuff he loved. The bridge from one to the other was crazy energy, focus, and unrelenting determination.

What happened:
- His mother had introduced something to him he became good at. None of their family had done dance, so it was sheer luck (or maybe she had seen something in him). Many kids go to dance school, but don't amount to much. They do it for a few years, as a hobby more than anything else – something to do on a Saturday morning. When they leave normal school they get a normal job, any dance aspirations they may have jettisoned for peanuts from paid employment [Their aspirations were weak or non-existent. Their parents never had any real dance expectations of them.] Our Kid though was different; he was good, really good, and he had real aspirations.

- A *negative* experience was the final push to change his life. Something bad was the seed for something good. Being too comfortable is deadly; people who are too comfortable don't change their lives. Change comes from desire, being 'satisfied' kills desire. This is why Gang Fit advises you to *go out and create hardship for yourself* if hardship doesn't find you. Hardship will kill you or make you change your life. One of the quickest ways to induce it is to quit your job now. Employment is a drug which murders self-improvement. Note: Steer clear of comfortably employed people, they exist in a different universe. They have nothing for you. Outside work they talk about normal shit; shit which has no bearing on creating something amazing. You can't tell them your aspirations, plans, and ambitions – they don't understand them. They are a drain on your energy. The foundation of their world is enslavement.

- He realized there was no point being a big fish in a small pond. The world can't be conquered that way. Being the captain of an ocean-going ship isn't the same as being the captain of a paper-boat on a puddle. So, he moved to the City. He didn't have much money, but that didn't stop him. Not having enough money is the most pathetic, bullshit reason that the majority of individuals use for why they can't get on.

- The environment he moved to was where the opportunities were. Looking for water in the desert is dumb. Move out the desert! Further, he met like-minded people with the same energy and drive as him. A virtuous circle.

- Whilst he was employed on jobs he still grew his own world. This is the opposite to what the normal person does – they're employed, and in their off time they watch Netflix. Their lives will always be in the hands of other people.

- The world is full of talented people who never get anywhere. I have met some of them (you will as well), they're pathetic - full of excuses and made-up reasons why they never amounted to much. They are sick making. Apparently, they had a more difficult time than anybody else, as if life had made *their* lives uniquely hard. They are neither self-aware nor aware of anyone else's life. Our Kid had a talent, what made him diverge from the unfulfilled talent was that *he never stopped.*

So, if you have come from a crap environment, full of hardship and negativity that comfortable people will never understand, you have been given a gift, a gift which is the fuel for your hatred, anger and dissatisfaction. It is the energy you need to conquer the world.

99 Cent Shop

If you visit New York (or any city), as well as doing the usual tourist stuff; go to the 99Cent stores. Hang around for a while. Look at the products on the shelves, What are they selling? What are people buying? What do the shoppers look like? What do the staff look like? What overall impression do you get? These places are fascinating – you can learn more here than at three years of university. Pick up a multi-pack of potato-chips and go through check-out. [You can feed them to the pigeons outside. The local authority doesn't like that; they view pigeons as no more than dirty tree-rats that spread germs. But have you ever caught a cold from a pigeon? Fuck no. Humans spread more germs. Pigeons are clever modern dinosaurs with personality – watch the interaction between them. You notice that some have rings around their legs?]

What you'll learn by going to these stores is difficult to say, but you'll learn something – something which should stick in your mind. It is fuel for your plans and ambitions. Here's the point: Very often the most important things can't be easily explained or written down like a 'how to guide'. It's the random shit that's important. If you want to be a writer, some morons will say, "take a writing course", as if that's going to help. Writing courses are for people whose writing is boring shit. If you want to be a writer, visit bars at 3am, strike up conversations with the regulars in greasy spoon diners, visit the Amazon rainforest, climb a mountain, fight with people, go to parties, visit prisons – all of that will make you a better writer than doing a writing course. In other words, the way to get somewhere or achieve something is not through the obvious predictable way. This is why a business degree won't make you any better at business - it doesn't cover the real realities of business.

****

As a thinking person you should have a love/hate view of the 99Cent Store. If you *only* hate them you're missing something about the richness of human life. If you *only* love them - you are going nowhere. Life should be viewed as an experiment - 99Cent stores are a petri-dish of humanity, a slice of life you can learn from. Some people will say that "viewing life as an experiment" is cold and heartless, they're idiots – taking yourself out of the equation and viewing the world through action, inaction, feedback and consequence is the way to change your world. *Creating a different life is driven by intense emotion, not lack of emotion* – you refuse to accept an enslaved existence. You think an Olympic athlete is emotionless? Of course not; desire is their rocket fuel - but they focus that desire into a training program, forensic in its application. Don't listen to people who say you're heartless if you *apparently* have no emotions, they're the shallow ones.

Two things which will help you to succeed in life are understanding yourself and understanding other people. Understanding doesn't mean that you empathise with people, why should you? Only that you understand why they think like they do, what motivates them (or doesn't). In the same way, you shouldn't *empathise with yourself*, that makes you someone who can't see the world for what it is. Don't feel sorry for yourself, or make excuses why you think, or do, dumb shit.

People visit the city and only see the tourist stuff, the good things – but this is only a small part of the real city. Visit the 99Cent stores.

The same principle applies to places where rich people shop. They're full of wankers – but they're fascinating, with cool things that money can buy, and people who are empowered by money. You should view those places the same way you view the 99Cent store. Everything is a learning opportunity.

TASK - For the next month visit places where people at the financial ends of the spectrum shop, eat, or collect in their clone-like groups. View them as data for analysis. Stop any emotions you have about these people; emotions colour your judgment. Most people been educated and brainwashed into thinking there is only the world of work and all that stuff. That exists, but its relevance to you is minimal; it is only one of a million worlds. As a young person you should see the worlds of other people. Expose yourself to their reality.

If you think you don't have enough money to go to places where rich people collect, you're wrong – you don't need money, just confidence. You can go to any rich shop, art gallery or similar, for free. Restaurants or clubs cost some money but you can spend the minimum amount. Warning: Don't suck up to wealthy people - that makes you a prick. You have no dignity. Even if you become wealthy, you'll still be a prick. You don't deserve Gang Fit. It will self-destruct in your hands.

Money is More Powerful Than Heroin – And You Know What People Do to Get Heroin

The first place I bought in the City was the size of postage stamp. I bought it via a crooked mortgage broker (they're all crooked). The finance industry is chock-full of criminals, bent as a fifteen-bob note. When you have an industry based on making money from giving other people money, even a monkey in a suit is given money. I found the broker through a crooked solicitor who owned fifteen properties which he was getting tax relief on, even though the Law was you could only claim tax relief on one property.

I was only young but realised the world outside school was nothing like they had taught me.

The flat I bought was in a shit part of the city. The only locals I liked were the foxes that regularly raided the rubbish bins. All the young guys owned 'devil dogs'. My next-door neighbour was a prostitute who kept open hours. All the shop fronts had metal grills. I left after a year. [Note: Only shit people like living in shit areas. There's no point living in a nice house if outside is drug and crime infested. If you grew up in an area like this, move out as soon as you can. It is far better having a crap property in a nice area than the reverse. If you live in a troubled area, the trouble will enter through your front door, walk up your stairs, and shit on your front room carpet – you won't be able to avoid it]

Some years and three properties later I wanted to buy a house, but I had no money and was 'unemployable'. I went to see a broker I had become friendly with, he worked for a well-known international finance company; "Hi, good to see you, how can I help?" "I need a mortgage for a house". He asked, "How much is it?" I told him I needed £300k but didn't earn a wage. "No problem. I can get it for you. You need three years self-employed accounts but I can sort that out for you".

A couple weeks later I was invited to posh place in an exclusive part of London where company directors, puffed-up business people, and entrepreneurs hang out. My broker friend introduced to an accountant he knew. After a half-hour chat and expensive coffees, the accountant said he would prepare some accounts for me. Easy as that. He was no doubt doing a favour for my broker friend, or getting a cut of the commission he would earn on the mortgage. I moved into the house eight weeks later. Everyone happy; me, the seller, the broker, the accountant, the solicitor (who did the *conveyancing*, a fancy word for 'money for old rope'), and, of course, the finance company (who had increased their assets and market share – the reason they overlook mortgage 'irregularities').

I could go on and on with stories like this.

Note: A market where everyone profits takes on a life of its own. It generates its own momentum. Part of that market will be based on fraud, an open secret overlooked by everyone with something to gain. The only thing which 'corrects' a market like this is some sort of Government intervention, reversal of confidence or zombie apocalypse. The experts who tell you, "the fundamentals are sound", are taking through their A-holes. There are *no fundamentals* in a market like this. Once you have enough money to buy (or credit finance) land and property as an investment, don't be a sucker and believe the ride will never reverse. Get *your fundamentals* right whatever the state of the market.

****

Money is a zillion times more powerful than heroin. It's the strongest drug in the world. The world is addicted to it. Every industry that deals with large amounts of money has corruption flowing through its veins. Any individual who has large amounts of money has done dodgy shit, lied, and hidden things from the law and tax agencies. Don't believe *anyone* who says they haven't. This isn't only people with a lot of money. Even the plumber, builder, taxi driver and gardener are evading as much tax as they can.

People *kill* to get money. People *prostitute* themselves to get money. People go to *prison* because of money. Friends and families *fall out* because of money. The ironic thing is that the pursuit of money creates slavery more than having money creates freedom. People are enslaved to money. It's the only addiction that all of society encourages.

Money has the power to transform your life in a good way *or* a bad way.

Negative:

1 You sell your soul, your principles, your mother, your positive relationships – to get it.

2 You are not grounded when you make it. You act like a prick. You think you're most important person on the planet. You waste it all on shit. This happens to some people who win the lottery; they go from zero, to hero, then back to zero. Essentially, they were always zero.

Positive:

1 As you earn/make it, you grow as a person. You learn your own strengths and weaknesses. You strengthen the relationships with people you care about.

2 The alleviation of the problems caused by poverty. You share it with the people and things you care about – you 'payback' the people who encouraged and supported you. You use it to improve your life and create opportunity for others.

3 Travel the world. Experience life in the way people without money can't. Live out your childhood dreams – cross the world's oceans in a boat; take a rocket to the moon; fishing for Mahseer in the rapids of an Indian river.

****

Some rich people say that "money doesn't make you happy". Take no notice of that, what the rich idiot really means is *money hasn't made them happy*. Money hasn't made them happy because they are not grounded individuals who know themselves. Money has the power to make you *very happy* if you're already a person who has sorted out their shit, come to terms with reality, and knows what's important. Money takes away all the problems that lack of money creates. That automatically makes you happier, but it won't bring back your dead child.

Having severe money problems is far better than having severe non-money problems. Sort out the important shit; money will be additive – it will make you happier. Don't sort out your shit – money will only make you happier for a while.

Garbage Protection Mechanism

All the world's oxygen comes from plants. All the world's bullshit comes from idiots. You need to protect yourself from idiots.

A mate who was in the South African army, told me about 'suppressing the enemy'. The military call it *suppressive fire* or *covering fire* - there are technical differences, but essentially it's a tactic for stopping the enemy from doing something; attacking, advancing, or trying to kill you or a member of your group. It involves bombarding extreme amounts of bullets or artillery at (or in the general direction of) the enemy. The shit-tonne of metal is so intense that the enemy doesn't dare poke its ugly head out of its cover, let alone return fire. This strategy is used *because it's effective*. That's all that matters. If it wasn't, the military wouldn't use it – those fuckers are pragmatic, they know the harsh reality of war, something the normal person has no concept of. Nice people get eaten up when things get nasty.

Childhood example: You know as a kid, when someone was lecturing you or talking rubbish, you put your fingers in your ears and started singing? The louder they spoke, the louder you sang? This was done for two reasons:

1 To block out their garbage

2 To *show them* you were blocking out their garbage

This was pretty effective, as well as being hilarious. Kids naturally know about the idea of suppression - the military didn't invent it.

There are times as adult when you should employ your *garbage protection strategies*. The aim is to stop a person bending your ear back with verbal garbage. Note: Suppression is just one strategy for stopping someone from doing something. There are others.

TASK – The next time someone is spewing bullshit in your direction, try these:

- Start humming to yourself
- Look them in the eyes for five seconds; slowly turn your head - walk away
- Pretend to have a heart attack
- Start choking
- Cough loudly in their face
- Suddenly shout, "Look at that!" whilst pointing to the sky. Then run off
- Start doing interpretive dance
- Punch them in the stomach
- Change the subject, when they're mid-sentence
- Pretend you've got a notification on your phone
- Say you need to visit the toilet urgently
- Hold your palm in front of their face ('talk to the hand')
- Most effective is just to tell them to "fuck off"

Whatever; enjoy yourself. Make up your own techniques. Don't be concerned with what the other person thinks - they're adding to the world's supply of bullshit, and harming the planet.

****

Some people say, "if you have to raise your voice when you argue, you've lost the argument". That's all well and good in their fantasy world, but it's tripe in the real world; the world where, 'he who uses greater force wins'. Sound is a force; it destroyed the Wall of Jericho. Really loud sounds make people cower; it stops them in their tracks. If shouting loud (and being 'aggressive') stops the bullshit of someone else, you have won, regardless of who is right or wrong. You have come out on top. People also say, "if you resort to violence you have lost the argument" - again, in reasonable world that may be right, but in the real world if someone is threatening, abusing or trying to intimidate you, and you give them a slap - you have won if it stops them.

Normal people who tell you how to behave are trying to control you – those same people will view what Gang Fit says as "encouraging violence". Listen, if you go round being verbally and physically aggressive to innocent people you are a moron; eventually you will pay for your stupidity; and you'll deserve it – you'll get nowhere in life. But it is perfectly acceptable to get physical, or show signs of aggression (i.e., make your feelings *unequivocally* clear) if people are trying to dominate and abuse you. In the situation where someone is potentially going to be violent to you or your loved ones, taking them out first *reduces* potential violence. Violence against them is far better than violence against you. Your fist will be a garbage disposal mechanism. Pretty obvious if you have a brain. Don't listen to people who don't know the realities of war.

Avoid, suppress, or neutralise the unwarranted garbage that comes in your direction. The bonus is that if you do it now, you'll get less of it in the future.

You Can Be a Flop

You see former elite athletes on television breaking down the technical reasons a current elite athlete is the best in the world. There are three problems with this: 1/ It doesn't take into account the thousands of athletes (who are 'invisible') who may have the same technique but are nowhere near the best in the world; 2/ at some stage a better athlete will come along a with a different technique; 3/ they may be the best in the world *in spite* of having a faulty technique. In other words, the elite athlete on TV is talking bullshit. Be careful believing 'experts'. It can make you an idiot.

In the track and field event of Shot Put there are two techniques for putting the shot, the glide and the spin. Whichever is used, the goal is to putt the shot with maximum velocity at the optimal angle of release (~ 45 degrees). Which technique the shot putter uses is dependent on their size and power; and their ability to perfect the more complicated spin technique. The point is that two *completely different techniques* are used for the same end – putting the shot as far as possible.

In tennis, there are three stances: closed, open and semi-open. Players use whatever one suits them. World-class players use different techniques for the same end; how the racquet face interacts with the ball. One could argue that a player may have been taught a particular technique (say, a single-handed backhand) but could have been better using a different technique (a double-handed backhand) – we'll never know. Some sprinters are *made worse* by the application of techniques and training which don't suit them. Destroyed by bad coaches.

****

At the 1968 Mexico Olympics, a little-known athlete, Dick Fosbury, took the athletics world by storm when he won the gold medal and broke the world record with a 2.24m (7ft 4ins) high jump. He had invented a technique which no other athlete was using. The *Fosbury Flop* is now is used by every competitive high-jumper in the World. Previous to this Fosbury had been a fucking average high jumper! At that time the three techniques used to clear the high jump bar were the scissors, western roll, and straddle jump.

Then this happened.

Up until the 1960s, high jump athletes had to land on hard ground (sand, sawdust or thin mats). This meant that, whatever technique was used to clear bar, athletes had to ensure they landed on their feet. However, Lady Fortuna favoured Fosbury when his high school became one of the first to install deep foam matting for the high jump landing. This change gave him the opportunity to try new ways to clear the bar without having to land on his feet. So, he used a technique which felt natural to him, and which he was good at – *a natural fit*. Instead of facing forwards, he used his opposite leg and jumped the bar backwards. He created athletics history, and went from a nobody to an Olympic gold medalist.

- Shot Put: Two techniques
- Tennis: Multiple techniques
- High Jump: A change in the 'environment' allowed for a different technique.

Note: Tumblers and acrobats can clear a high jump bar well over the world record height. However, the rules of the event don't allow for two-footed take-offs. If the rules were changed a whole new technique and type of athlete would dominate. Despite what people tell you, there are no rules in real life – just action, inaction, reaction, and feedback.

The point is:

1 Find what you're good at
2 If you can't find it, create it
3 If you're not good at anything (very unlikely), get good at something
4 A change in circumstances creates opportunities – some may happen to suit your talents. Keep your eyes open
5 Respect ways of doing things, but don't be limited by them. Sport has multiple techniques for getting things done. How many techniques and ways do you think *real life* has?
6 Smash up low-level people who say *you* can't achieve something. They're keeping you down. Your worst enemy.

Vegetables are Poison

Many vegetables taste like vomit. You've been told to eat them because "they're good for you". They contain vitamins, minerals, fibre, and other beneficial and brain boosting trace elements. Well, this may be true but it's only half the story. They are also poison.

All plants are engaged in a form of chemical warfare because, like all living things, they want to pass on their DNA. This is contained in the fruit, flower, nut, or seed. The plant will encourage the animals or insects that help in this process and discourage the animals that harm it. The encouragement is in the form of sweet tasting fruit, nectar and so on. The discouragement in the form of foul, bitter tasting or poisonous leaves. Some animals have developed digestive processes that neutralise the toxins whereas others may be harmed by them. Sometimes animals will purposely eat a plant they wouldn't normally eat to make themselves sick if they have a stomach bug.

Brain-dead nutritionists, dieticians and health experts go on about the benefits of vegetables without realising that part of those benefits come from the small amounts of poison or toxins they contain which makes our body stronger. The reverse is also true, some people cannot tolerate the natural 'pesticides', anti-feedants and phytochemicals in certain vegetables. Once again, we have example of what you're being taught at school, college, or in your nutrition module at university, making you an educated idiot, unable to see the complete picture. Vegetables are good for some people, harmful to others. Forget about the experts who say they're good for you because of this or that reason.

The next time someone dishes you up inedible cabbage, ask them "why the fuck have you put that *poison* on my plate!"

True Story

There was this kid. He was very fast. He was the fastest kid in his primary school. Then he was the fastest kid in his high school. Then he was the fastest kid in the city. Then he was the fastest junior sprinter in the country. Then he was the fastest junior sprinter of all-time in the country. By the time he was a senior sprinter he had run 10.15 seconds for 100 metres. He was super-fast. If he had been a footballer, rugby player, NFL star or baseball player – he would have been the fastest in the world in those sports. But he was a sprinter. He had a bedroom full of medals and trophies. His parents had the most important ones on the mantelpiece in their front room. They were proud of him. He thought the world was his oyster. He was still only 21.

He trained hard for the next three years but his 100m time didn't improve; if anything things got worse; he was getting injuries and niggles. He began to realise he was near the limits of his ability. He had one or two faster wind-aided times (not allowable in the rules of competition), which gave him the feeling of what it was like to run near 10 seconds flat. This kept him going in the hope that he would run just as fast with a legal wind. He never did. He was still fast enough to represent his country at the Olympics – the pinnacle of an athlete's life. One day he got the call-up to wear his country's vest. He'd come a long way since running against his mates at primary school.

Now he was at the Olympics. He easily made it through the early heats. He got through to the quarter-finals. The tension and excitement was building. Like many athletes at the Olympics, he couldn't sleep. In the quarters he just managed to scrape through as a fastest loser; he had messed up the start (normally his strong point), this had put him a metre behind - but he kept relaxed and focused, and regained some of the lost ground. What a relief!

Two days later he was in his blocks at the start line of the Summer Olympics 100m semi-final, the biggest moment in his career. The starter's gun went off, he got a great start. He accelerated smoothly and came upright slowly, like a plane taking off. He was running well. Then something he had never experience before happened. At 40 metres one of the competitors rocketed past him as if he was standing still. What the fuck; what the *actual fuck*?! The guy was creating a bigger gap every second, there was nothing our sprinter could do – he just kept repeating in his head, "stay relaxed, stay relaxed; concentrate on your own race!" However, he had tightened up - this made him slow down; only a little, but enough to make him feel he was battling his own body. His finishing time was 10.25, not bad under the circumstances, but he hadn't qualified for the final. The winner of the race (who went on to win the gold medal) had run a *mind-bending 9.68 seconds* – over half a second faster, and fifteen feet ahead.

Half a second is a chasm in the 100m sprint. Competitively, it's a different beast.

This one experience smashed our sprinter. He realized he would never achieve that sort of level. He had witnessed the pinnacle of sprinting and it wasn't him - he wasn't even fucking close. What was the point of sweating blood; killing himself in all weathers, just to run 10flat? Even *that* wasn't guaranteed.

He was only 25 years old when he quit. Even though he had a career that most sprinters would die for, and a house full of trophies to show for it, he felt like a loser – *he didn't even feel fast anymore.*

****

In your quest to conquer the world, remember you are conquering *your* world. What other people do is none of your business. It's out of your control. You are creating something unique to you. When you start diverging from the pack, some of your friends won't like it, it sticks in their throat that you are doing well, not them. Now, the same goes for you; there will *always* be someone more successful, better looking, better at sport; a better artist, a better singer - someone with a better physique, whatever. That's life. That doesn't make you a loser

The fool wants status, but they'll always be someone with a higher status. You shouldn't be bothered about status. If you meet someone who tries to laud their status over you, feel free to smash them up. That will knock the 'status' out of them.

Postscript: After a few years, our sprinter came to terms with his experience – he wasn't a loser. Sprinting had given him a good life. He had met all sorts of wonderful people; it had taken him around the world. He'd had the privilege to represent his country in the world's most prestigious sporting event. That was the past – now, he had a new life ahead of him.

Physical Standards

These targets are straightforward and no bullshit. They're not complicated. These are not elite standards, but achieving all five would likely take you into the top 1% of the population. You'd be in tremendous physical shape.

1 **Deadlift**: One-rep max of 2 x body weight (general strength)

2 **Chin-ups**: 20 (usable upper body strength)

3 **100m sprint**: Under 13 seconds (speed)

4 **One mile**: Under 6 minutes (endurance)

5 **Body-fat**: 10-12% - a six-pack is just visible (health)

The most challenging for an older person (60yrs+) to achieve is a sub-13sec sprint; sub-14secs would be more appropriate (the others are not *too* difficult). Retaining the ability, as you age, to generate dynamic muscular contractions provides solid information about the general physical state of the muscles, tendons, ligaments and nerves. If you can do it *without a warm-up*, even better. Being able to turn on strength, quickness and agility without any warm-up is the pure expression of youth.

There are different health tests a person can do: In a *clinic/lab* – blood tests, biomarker tests, blood pressure, heart rate, scans; in a *gym* - stress tests, body fat, VO2 max, and so on. That's all well and good, but these five simple performance tests you can do yourself and are easy to measure. Physical performance is an excellent indicator of the general health of the body.

There is no point adding in more target categories – vertical high jump, rowing ability, back-flips, and so on, as it's the *engine* in the car that ultimately determines performance not what the car can be used for. The five categories give us a global view of the state of the 'engine'. That's enough.

****

Dynamic strength and physical health not only help you cope with one-off short-term emergences; you're being chased by zombies, Arsenal fans or the Fuzz, but also with foreseeable and unforeseeable long-term risks. The foreseeable long-term risk is old age and all the illness and negative health shit that comes with it. Note: Even though old age is foreseeable (barring accidents, lion attacks, and deadly viruses) and will happen to the majority of people – most individuals ignore it, then those fuckers are surprised when they get a heart attack. Unforeseeable long-term risks are just that – maybe a volcano eruption, meteor strike, nuclear war; who knows?

Short-term risks we can all understand. Long-term risks many people tend to ignore. The way to see what the long-term health risks are is to look at people older than yourself. What do they look like? There's your long-term risk. Good health is your risk reduction. It's your Life Insurance Policy. Your physical ability to cope with everyday life and extreme events, fights, disasters and war is *essential*. The robustness of a biological system is marked by its ability to cope with (or thrive from) variation. Life is a stress test; age is a stress test, random events are stress tests. Banks are subject to stress tests to see if they can cope with fluctuations and extreme situations. If the banks fail the test they are instructed to increase their cash reserves, so they can ride out any future storm. Your 'reserves' to survive life's stress tests are physical strength and robust health.

Many physically lazy, weak and unfit people can cope when times are comfortable; they've engineered their lives around comfort. But when some extreme shit hits the fan, which it *always* does, they're dead. The body can't cope; it's pushed beyond its abilities.

1st Law of Cybernetics

In his book, *An Introduction to Cybernetics* (1956), Ross Ashby introduced his *'Law of Requisite Variety'*. This is the 1st Law of Cybernetics. Ashby was primarily interested in homeostasis; the way in which complex systems, operating in changing environments, succeed in maintaining equilibrium within tightly defined limits. Simply put, his law proposed that if a system is to be able to deal successfully with the diversity of challenges that its environment produces, then it needs to have a range of responses which is (at least) as varied as the problems thrown up by the environment. You can

97

see how this applies to our own capabilities. In order to be able to deal with the variety of challenges and events that life presents, you need to have physiological, metabolic, nervous and psychological systems which have the capability to cope with variation and random events.

Again: Only having a physically comfortable life means you will get wiped out in an emergency because your body has lost its ability to deal with anything uncomfortable. You need to purposely add in 'extremes' - high intensity training, resistance work, high heart rates, and other physically demanding activities.

****

Unless you are training for a competitive sport you don't need to do as much as you think for outstanding health. Doing too much will mean you get the 'plods' – you'll have no physical or mental energy, and your legs will feel heavy and sore. That's no state to be in. The whole point about exercise is that you should feel super-great most of the time not super-fatigued. This is rarely a problem that arises for the normal person. Joe Public are physically lazy, they do anything to avoid physical discomfort. But if you're *really* motivated, make sure you don't go overboard. Training for competitive sport is different; you have to bust your balls, almost to the point of falling apart (which is what eventually happens to all long-term athletes).

Warning: *Do not become a health and exercise bore.* Boring people deserve to be locked in prison. They kill happy people with their monotonous shit. Listening to a boring person is a window into what death must be like. Being fit, strong, dynamic and healthy is fucking great, meaning you can exterminate morons, Z's, idiots and wage-slaves, but don't spend all your life in a gym or looking at yourself in the mirror. The rest of life needs you.

If you are young your body has superhuman abilities that older people no longer have. Build muscle, eat good food, get strong and sprint! If you stick by these, not only will you be in the top 1% of the population, but by the time you're old you will seem like a genetic freak to the lazy, fat, and unfit people around you. Their brains won't be able to compute it; they'll say you're "lucky". But in the immortal words of Mickey Mouse (don't quote me), "the harder you work the luckier you get".

If Things Are Bad, Make Them Worse

CHALLENGE - *If you're on welfare, get off as soon as you can.*

Gang Fit has nothing against free money. Only an idiot doesn't like free money. If people, government or tax payers are stupid enough to give out free money that's their problem - you shouldn't care about that. Everyone wants money. What's wrong with getting it for as little as possible? Some idiots say, "you should be concerned about personal dignity", and not claim money off the state – ignore them. If it's legal, you claim it; fuck personal dignity as they see it. Oh, "earn money for a hard day's work!" Shut up, wage slave. Politicians, investors and all sorts of people get loads of money for practically nothing, they don't feel guilty about it, but they tell you about getting a few quid from the State? *Welfare is bad because free money comes with a cost, it makes most people lazy.* They get up late, watch mid-morning TV, play video games, and fart about aimlessly. A wasted life.

The saying goes, "Hell is working most of the time to have just enough money to be broke". There's no doubt about that. But an equal hell is having just enough welfare to keep you alive. If you can't get off welfare because you can't find a job or think of any ideas to make money, you should sign off. You should turn a bad (but survivable) situation into a *much worse situation* – this will hit you like an electric shock, and engage a desperate motivation. It's frightening but very effective; you'll have to find something or you don't eat. The reason people can't get off welfare is they are comfortably uncomfortable, they can just about survive. So they don't try hard enough. There is *always* a way to earn or make money, unless you live on an island only inhabited by Penguins. Signing-off focuses your mind.

If welfare doesn't make you lazy, *really* doesn't, then claim it whilst you are unemployed. It's nothing to be ashamed about, it's only money. Trapped people, working people, business people, taxpayers – all the normies tell you it's shameful - but don't care what they think. All creatures on the planet want to get food for as little effort as possible - in the human world, money is food. You'd be an idiot to refuse it if there were no negative effects. Regard it as a grant or investment in your time. Whilst you're claiming you have time to pursue and develop other things. The idea of a Universal Basic Income is just that; giving people free money, no questions asked - allowing the unemployed to invest their time developing other interests. The fear is that people won't do anything and just live off UBI. That's most likely true. Most people aren't interested in putting in effort to improve their lives.

Ultimately, the only problem is if free money makes you lazy and stops you progressing; if it does, then you need to make conditions harder by not accepting it. If it doesn't stop you from pursuing your plans, schemes and crazy ideas then take it. This is called being pragmatic. Don't listen to the emotional reactions of zombies. Do what is right for you.

"If things are bad, make them worse". Translated: If you are comfortable just surviving, your life is going nowhere. It's mindboggling how many people stay in a poverty stricken existence – lacking the motivation and energy to get out of it. These people live a useless and ineffective life, no use to themselves or anyone else. If you have the scarcity, just surviving, mindset, you need to do something to knock yourself out of it or your life will slowly turn to shit. Purposely create even more hardship; either you die or start sorting your life out. To cure a situation which is bad but tolerable, you need to make it intolerable.

A Property Buys You a Car – A Car Doesn't Buy You a Property

One dollar when you're young is worth twenty when you're old.

It is better to have a million quid when your twenty-five than a hundred million when you're seventy. When you're twenty-five you have physical energy, you can enjoy life in a way that no old person, however rich, can. Yeah, yeah, older people may have different priorities and get fulfillment from different things; things that a young person is oblivious to, but there are few old fossils who wouldn't want to be physically younger, healthier and more robust. Old people who say they wouldn't are liars - they're like fat people who say they are happy being fat. Youth is the most powerful super-drug; you hardly need sleep yet you wake up looking like you spent the preceding day at an alpine health spa. By the time you're an old, this reverses - you *may* have been to an alpine health spa but you wake up looking like a bear sat on your face.

To enjoy your youth, go to parties, travel, hit gym, doss about, and do "stupid shit" (it's not stupid shit). But this is what you need to do; you need to combine having fun with making money, setting up some sort of business, buying property or land, or learning to be an expert at something. People say it's good to get to know people who've achieved success in their lives. True. But once you start achieving things for yourself, those people will start appearing, as if by magic, you won't need to look for them.

****

After leaving university, a friend of mine went to work for a well-known investment bank. After 18 months or so he realised that although he would be financially secure if he stayed at the bank, he would end up dissatisfied with life. He looked at the older employees who'd worked there for years – even though they were *very* comfortably off they were out of shape and burnt out. They looked half-dead. He didn't want to be like that. Being a courageous individual he decided he would try to raise some money from his associates and clients, and go it alone in property development. He wrote up a plan and managed to persuade enough people to part with their money in return for a predicted profit [Note: This could have gone tits-up; he could have lost his and other people's money]. He had already bought his first property (as an investment) when he was eighteen; mostly using the money he inherited after his father committed suicide. Even at eighteen he was clued-up. Both his parents had built businesses, so it was natural for him to put his money into something that would give him a return. They never brainwashed him into the idea of getting a job, like most zombie parents do. The normal teenager would have wasted the money on a car, encouraged by their parents – "now you don't need to rely on me and your Dad to ferry you around!" If you are young and receive a substantial sum of money, do not waste all of it on a fucking car! A car is the opposite of an investment, *it takes money out of your pocket* – don't be like the normal young person, they are trainee slaves, surrounded by slaves, with slaves as parents. They consume rather than create.

Anyway, back to my friend. With the money he raised he bought a commercial property, then another, and another. Other people saw this and paid him to work on development projects. He could ask for as much pay as he wanted as he had the ability to raise lots of money. The more he said he was too busy to work for others, the more they offered to pay him. He worked only one-quarter of the time but got paid three times as much. In-between contracts he would spend months off, travelling the world and experiencing life. He had escaped. However, he set up his own property development company, financing big commercial and private housing projects.

Now, he's loaded of course. He only gets involved in projects he's interested in, and spends most of his time travelling and enjoying life. He realised early on *what he didn't want* - a life of employment. So he created his own version of reality.

****

It normally takes a while to make money. Along the way you will have to be able to put up with crushing pressure and frustration. I have glossed over my friend's rise to multimillionaire; he had many sleepless nights. I don't know whether he had any self-doubts, maybe he did, but it didn't stop him. You are not successful once you've made a shitload of money, that's bullshit – you are successful as soon as you start creating a different world for yourself. That's where it begins. So, whilst you're having fun, going out and getting pissed, you should also be doing something which makes you diverge from the rest of the crowd. The rest of the crowd are going nowhere except wage-slavery. Teenagers and young people want to fit in and be part of a tribe; that is there undoing – they brainlessly follow the fads and fashions of their time. This is the normal shit, it isn't clever or original. What's original is the young person who has the sense to realise that clones their age will achieve nothing of substance. They see that the 'vitalness' of the youth generation turns to the reality of wage entrapment. The unusual young person is the one who has the foresight to understand they need to begin building something for themselves.

Start something now, not mañana. You don't want to wait until you're half-dead before you have money. Despite what the tabloids and sensible people tell you, being young and having lots of money is a dream – it's your reward for being different.

If you live in the City, think twice before buying a car. If your transport is a way of earning money or starting a business, all well and good – if not, it's a waste of money. "Yeah, but a car gives me independence, and I have fun times!" This is the utterance of a zombie, not a person with an independent mind. If you can't find any friends who don't have the same attitude as you, don't let them waste your time with nonsense. It's great to have friends but there's a time for play and a time for work. Doing your own thing isn't boring, it's exhilarating. When your first successes come in you feel like a king.

All of Life in One Day

School teaches you rules (ways to act). In real life there are no rules, only lessons – those lessons will determine *your own rules*.

At school, you are not allowed to hit a bully – this is bad education both for you *and* the bully. In real life you are entitled to hit someone who is physically threatening you. In real life the bully will find out the real consequence of being a bully; a smashed-up face.

At school, the losers in a race get a clap (or even a medal), "Oh, well done Maximillian for putting in so much effort!" In real life no one cares about the loser, no matter how much effort they put in. Putting in effort is a great thing, but no one is going to give you credit for writing a shit book for example) because you put in effort.

School tells you it's bad to skip lessons or take time off during term; "it harms your education" – as if school invented the idea of learning. In real life, education can come from anywhere.

School doesn't prepare you for the real world. When you leave schol your proper education begins. Additionally, you may learn the most important life-lesson in one glorious, or awful, day.

Muscular Arms

More than anything else skinny arms make you look like a weakling - and when you look like a weakling some idiots will try to push you around. Most kids with thin arms hate wearing t-shirts because it makes them feel puny. If your arms look like toothpicks and *you don't feel puny*, Gang Fit can't help you. You have no shame.

Ectomorphs are particularly prone to having thin arms. But if you're an ectomorph there is no reason why you should continue looking like a stick insect. You're probably stronger than you look, which ain't much as you look weak. The good news is, if you have naturally thin arms, but self-respect, you can add on enough quality muscle so that after a year of training, *you'll find any excuse to show them off* - "look at these guns, motherfuckers!"

There are hundreds of arm exercises but you can build tremendously strong and impressive looking arms by using just three basic exercises - ones that have stood the test of time; *chin-ups, parallel-bar dips* and *press-ups*. The key is, you've got to put in tremendous effort. If you blitz your arms for six months they will grow muscular and strong, like steel; doesn't matter if you are "naturally skinny". There is no need to get caught up in what type of exercise is better for your arms; this is focusing on the wrong thing. If the ten most important things for growing muscular arms were listed, numbers one to nine would be *intensity; raw, blood-boiling, intensity.* Most gym bunnies don't realize that working your arms hard has a similar feeling to working your legs hard – it's painful, your heart rate rockets and you feel spaced-out. Yes, just from working the arms.

["Hard-Gainers" aren't really hard-gainers, they're 'easy exercisers', they don't work hard enough. Some people *do* gain muscle more easily than others, that's a fact - but let's reframe it, we can call them 'easy-gainers' – you are a *normal-gainer*, not a hard-gainer. Get that self-defeating crap out of your mind]

You can train to get strong or you can train to get muscular. If you have thin arms you should train for muscle - of course you will get stronger, *far* stronger, but the emphasis should be to *grow muscle*. This (generally) means doing sets of medium to high reps, not low reps. Low: 1-5 reps. Medium: 8-12 reps. High: 15+ reps. This doesn't mean that it's easier, quite the reverse, it's harder. Training a few reps takes tremendous effort but doesn't have anywhere near the gut-wrenching fatigue of higher reps to failure.

The formula for arm growth is regular hard training interspersed with *shock training*. People are confused, *progression* is more important than regular progressive overload training. *Progression is the goal; 'progressive overload' is a routine.* See the difference? The idea of progressive overload is less convincing once you've been training for a while. It assumes you can work hard and keep on adding small amounts of weight once a week, once every two weeks, once a month, whatever. It sounds good in theory but eventually it hits the buffers. Gym turkeys do this stuff for years but never improve after initial gains. So, it's necessary to inject some *seriously hard work*. Don't get this wrong; regular progressive training is the bread and butter of strength and muscular improvements, the majority of gym users can't even do that! There is no need for them to do shock training – they just need to be consistent and work hard.

Regular training

1 Hard work
2 Consistency
3 Recovery
4 Enough sleep
5 Eat well

These are the main components of regular training.

Note: Even if you don't eat well, if you get enough calories you will still grow muscle – it won't be good for your long-term health, but you will get bigger (and maybe put on more fat). If you don't have enough calories, even if you eat well, muscle growth is difficult. For *overall health* it is best to eat well and eat enough!

Basic design - *using only the three exercises* (if you're not sure how to perform them, look on the internet):

Tuesday

Press-ups x 20 to 50 (i.e., whatever you can do)
Chin-ups x 10-25
Dips x 10-30

Do this all the way through, with only a few seconds between each exercise to regain your breath and composure. This is called a *superset*. Repeat twice with 3 minutes between sets.
Friday

Dips: 4 sets x 10 reps with as much added weight as you can handle
Chin-ups: 4 sets x 10 reps (as above)
Press-ups: 200 in total, in as few sets as you can

Have enough rest between sets to allow you to complete the next set. You don't need half a day! Unlike Tuesday's superset session you are completing all the dips first, then the chins, and lastly, the press-ups.

See how basic this is? You expected a fucking science manual? People like to overcomplicate gym workouts, when what they should be doing *is working very hard and being consistent.* Some gym experts will say that you should do this or that; "this hits the lower biceps...triceps near the elbows...develops a nice peak...works the entire muscle belly..." - forget all that nonsense, it's for nerds, not you. The different effects of these exercises are minimal; you just want to get muscle on your pipes. Don't be a knob, simple basics are good. It's built battleship bodies.

Note: This is only part of a total body work-out. Your arms will also be worked from rows, deads, press, and so on. There is no need to do more for them. This is more than enough. Stick to this routine for at least six-months before you introduce shock training - if you work like you mean it your arms will get bigger and stronger. You may need a week off every now and then (within reason) for extra recovery – that's fine. You'll crush the session on your return.

Shock training

When you're near your genetic potential for a body part, or you want to focus on a lagging area, it's a mistake to mindlessly stick to your regular training. You need to take that specific body part and murder it with *intensity and volume.* This extra stimulus will force your body to adapt. Regular training has a breadth vs depth trade-off. Working on your whole body is essential, but if you have skinny arms which are hardly improving, you need to specifically target them. If you do it seriously, it necessarily means you will have to reduce training for the other areas; but don't worry, a minimal amount of work will retain those, freeing up psychological and physical energy for your guns.

1 Concentrating on only one area (your arms) allows a greater improvement in that area than would be achieved by training all areas concurrently

2 Shock training *is not* for all year-round training but for a specific period, for a specific reason.

3 Shock training introduces variety into your training. It's easy to get stale – you end up going through the motions, not improving. Introducing the extra stimulus of a challenge, revitalises your workout.

4 This type of training is fearsome; it involves hurting yourself repeatedly. Your muscles and brain are telling you to stop, but something deep down, something primal, something without a name, *will not take orders from your weaknesses.* You leave your session feeling fucked but knowing you've just conquered the planet.

105

Note: Massive body builders work at an intensity that most people can't conceive of. Their regular training *is* shock training – it's brutal. There is no way you can do that. They are juiced-up-to-the-gills genetic freaks. They live, breath, eat, and shit, training. This sort of thing would cause the normal person to self-destruct. Be strategic, use shock training wisely. Only experience will teach you how far you can push it.

****

If a Hollywood producer said to you, "Hey, we want you for our new alien smashing-up action movie. We start shooting in two months - but you need bigger arms", would you do normal training or shock training? There's only one answer. To ensure you got the role you would have to blitz your arms practically every day (and eat far more protein). If you want to put one, two, or even three inches on your arms as *quickly as possible,* imagine there was a film contract and $15million dependent on it. Would you do it? What the fuck! Of course you would.

Having "naturally skinny arms" is not a barrier to strong muscular arms.

CHALLENGE 1 – One thousand press-ups in a day: Split your day into 10 x 1hour segments. Each hour aim to complete 100 press-ups. How you want to achieve the hourly total is up to you; 25 every 15 minutes or 10 every 6mins; whatever. Advice: Don't do more than 50% of the maximum amount of press-ups you can do in any one go, i.e. if your all-out max is thirty don't do more than fifteen. If you go for max every time your arms will be obliterated after four or five hours. The object is to complete the challenge, not to do a lot quickly then die.
One hundred press-ups an hour might not sound like much, but after six or seven hours the muscle fatigue in your triceps may mean that you'll start falling behind; in which case you'll have to carry over into eleven or twelve hours. If this is too easy for you, double it. Currently the 24hr world record is 46,001, which is one every two seconds; but I've watched videos of press-up 'records', they are complete hogwash, none of them are proper press-ups. Two full press-ups every two seconds for 24hrs is impossible, only a robot or super-alien could do that. Don't be a dick-splat, do *proper press-ups*. Doing loads of shit press-ups makes you look like a jerk.

Once you've completed this challenge try dips and chin-ups. This will be far harder for most people. But challenges should be difficult, right?

CHALLENGE 2 – *Shock training*: Choose two exercises, one for biceps, the other for triceps. Every day for one month do one hundred of each. Split each exercise into 10x10, alternating between biceps and triceps. I did this challenge after a friend suggested it. The result was remarkable – a whole extra inch on my upper arms, and thicker more muscular forearms. The average gym trainer takes a year to get that.

106

Make it difficult, but achievable, by choosing two demanding exercises; chin-ups and parallel bar dips will be enough for most people. As the days progress it naturally gets easier, so you'll need to reduce the time between sets, or add resistance (buy a weight belt or devise a way to add weight – be creative). What happens as the days pass is that the post-workout soreness gets less, but the stiffness increases, to a point. Be prepared for your arms to be rock-fucking-solid for the whole month. You may get one or two niggles, don't worry, don't be weak, carry on.

All training is ultimately psychological, it's your mind which pushes you – it overcomes your physical frailties. As the days pass you will look forward to this session more and more, not because it's easy but because it's a challenge, because it's hard, because you are doing what no one else is doing – it's your house of pleasure and pain. You will literally see your arms developing every day. After you have completed this challenge don't go straight back into regular arm training, take a week off.

Note: Whether you're at college or work, that is no excuse not to do this – everyone will wonder what you're up to. If you're at school and your clueless teacher tells you to stop, inform them that you're conducting a task set by **Gang Fit**, far better than the pointless crap they give you.

****

Some people say that being obsessed with your arms isn't for real athletes or trainers – ignore this. Whilst it's true that the legs, back and glutes (backside) are the foundation of real strength, what you should be concerned about is what makes you more capable for the various situations of real life. Being strong in the lower body, but weak in the upper body won't get you anywhere; the body is used as a whole for most everyday challenges. Not being able to hang, grip, or pull yourself up using only your arms will severely limit your abilities. Climbing buildings, trees, buildings, rock faces; whatever, demands that you have good upper body relative strength. Develop the ability to climb a thirty-foot rope using arms only – don't be like the weaklings who need to use their legs.

Final note: *Only* developing your body and nothing else is for losers; you see these types in the gym during the week - big guys with small prospects. The reason they are in the gym all day is because they have nothing else in life. Don't be a loser – exercise will not make up for a shit life which is going nowhere. Health and strength without freedom, independence and liberty, just makes you a fit slave.

Hippopotomonstrosesquippedaliophobia

One thing which will make you seem intelligent is knowing the meaning of words. This doesn't mean you will necessarily be more intelligent, but you'll be perceived (by most people) as intelligent. I was never a stupid kid but one day I realised that I didn't know the meaning of words, so I decided that I'd look up the definition of every word I didn't know. Because you know lots of words it doesn't mean you know what you're talking about (there are plenty of people who sound intelligent but talk crap), only that you know what *other* people are talking about. [I knew a guy who was useless at reading and writing, absolutely terrible, but that didn't stop him becoming a scrap metal dealer, and eventually a successful trader. He couldn't write for shit, yet he bought and sold big metals contracts]

TASK – For the next year, and in a less intense way for the rest of your life, every time you see, hear, or read a word you don't know the meaning of, look it up. If someone says something in conversation (a word or a phrase) which you don't understand, ask them what it means. Don't be a knob and pretend you have understood a word when someone uses it in conversation – it's *always* obvious when someone pretends they've understood something they don't understand. Don't do it!

A friend of mine recently learned the word *plethora*. Because he had just learnt it, the numbskull started using it everywhere; "a plethora of people"; "a plethora of exercises"; "a plethora of ducks" – stupid shit like that. It was funny though; it was obvious he had just learnt it.

1 Look up the definition of words you don't know
2 When you've learnt a word, don't keep using it like parrot
3 The dictionary definition of a word and its use in common parlance (look it up) are slightly different. Learn how the word is used properly

Will knowing more words give you a greater chance of succeeding in life? The jury's out. But at least you'll be able to understand what you hear and read, and you'll come across as more intelligent. Of course, if you're the world's fastest person it doesn't matter if you don't know the meaning of Hippopotomonstrosesquippedaliophobia.

Leave School at 3 - Leave Work at 5

School is a brainwashing device to prepare kids for work. Some schools even extend their hours - they finish at 5pm to replicate work hours. Wankers. The purpose of school is to educate kids to accept their world, not your world. At 3pm you see all the kids leaving the school gates; some get picked by parents, others catch the bus, or the train; some walk home (this is where the commute begins); others collect in the high street.

They think they're free. They view adults as bores who've never been young. But the joke's on them. 95% of them will end up the same way as the typical adult. They are clueless that they are being groomed for the world of employment. Education's ultimate aim is to produce work fodder. The government wants you to be a willing worker – they go on about "full employment", the definition of hell for a free person. *Full employment,* translated means full-slavery. Rise above this system as soon as you can. Leave them to their lives. Create your own life – free from the oblivion of full employment, the real purpose of school.

Purpose

You still get to do some unpleasant work when you're self-employed, but what you are not doing is purposeless work. This is the difference between being employed and doing your own thing. The work may be the fucking same but now it has a meaning.

A purposeless life is not worth living. It is hell on earth. An incarcerated man feeding a bird through the window of his cell; a person tending their garden; a young person training towards their vision of Olympic Gold – they have purpose. This is the difference between a labourer building a wall and the religious man building the wall of a church…one of them has a reason beyond a wage. There only needs to be ONE thing that gives your life purpose, that is enough. You could be an artist, writer, fighter, entrepreneur, brain surgeon, dancer, business owner, traveler, whatever – you have purpose. Doing something which has purpose frees the imprisoned man.

The Illustrated Man

'The Illustrated Man' is a collection of science fiction short stories, written by Ray Bradbury in 1951. It's fucking brilliant. Bradbury was a science fiction genius. Check him out. The 'illustrated man' himself is a vagrant former member of a carnival freak show with a heavily tattooed body. His tattoos, created by a time-travelling woman, are individually animated – each tells a different tale.

Fight anyone who says otherwise; all of Bradbury's stories were essentially about the human condition. He just played it out on a cosmic scale, with aliens, advanced technology and futuristic shit.

All *your* experiences are 'tattooed' on you. They are your scars and the lines on your face. The older you get, the more you will collect. This is called experience. Your tattoos will tell your story. If you live a brave, heroic and independent life - you become the illustrated man. Your stories will be imprinted on you; they *become* you, and you become them. If you have the curse of a comfortable and uneventful life, you hardly have any stories to tell, you're not fully developed.

Exposing yourself to the creative and destructive forces of nature - outside the usual life of employment, a monthly salary and soul-destroying monotony, will *create* you like the heat of a furnace creates steel. This is *good*, not bad. You will have legendary stories to tell.

****

An experienced woodsman can tell from the cross-section of a tree, its age, the climatic changes over its life, the soil conditions, diseases, infections and other environmental stresses. Above a certain threshold, events are imprinted on the tree. There is nothing wild and elemental...no living creature, which has perfect unblemished growth. All living things suffer stress, accidents, and random events – that's real life. Not only should you not avoid stress, you have to run towards it, it's where opportunity lies, and how your life is made.

If someone took a cross-section of you when you die, what are they going to see?

Ray Bradbury's, Illustrated Man, was a vagrant and a 'freak' – this is the risk you take. But only employed simpletons separate the heroic losers from the heroic winners.

The System

Here's the system that is designed to control you - then punish you, if act out of order.

1 They convince you that you need to be employed, creditworthy, and that you need a mortgage to buy a house.

2 If you act 'out of line' they make it difficult for you to be employed, get credit, and get a mortgage to buy a house.

They control you via your credit record and your 'criminal record'. Now a *non-hate crime* is recorded against you and can stop you getting a job. That's fucked-up. If you can't see that's warped, then you've been fucked-up. They brainwash you to believe in a system, then they make it difficult to be part of that system. That's sadism. They're sick. It's the same dynamic as a drug pusher creating an addict then withholding the drug to punish that addict.

You can't do anything to change the system. But once you step out of it, it becomes laughable; they can no longer control you with threats of withholding this or taking away that. People can only be controlled through fear. When you no longer care about their system, they are powerless. A side-effect is that you no longer care about the concerns of the normal person, because their concerns are nothing, just the emitted methane of people who don't realised they are caged. Well, they may realise but they are too weak and scared to do anything about it. Before any fuckers say this is self-centered, "you should care about other people!" - understand that those people don't give a shit about *your* problems, why should they? You're only returning the favour.

Discount

<u>TEST</u> - The next time you buy a medium (or more) priced good from a shop, ask for a 20% discount. Repeat this for the next ten items you buy. Training shoes, clothes, a microwave, fridge, phone – stuff like that. People don't ask for discounts for two reasons; 1/ they don't realize that stores will often consider discounts if it means getting a sale; 2/ they are too embarrassed to ask – they're meek. The ironic thing is that people save their money for sales, when they could be getting sale prices outside the sales if they had the confidence to ask. Once you've asked for a discount a few times, you get used to it.

When you branch out on building your own empire, you must be prepared to look stupid to other people; you must also be prepared to look as if you have no money. You *may* have no money until your successes start piling up, but you're going to have to divorce what the morons think of you – what matters is what you think of yourself. When you ask for a discount the shop assistant may think you're a loser, even though *they are one a shit wage*. How funny is that? [Note: that is why the butler is often more of a snob than the butler's boss]. Not only are they on a shit wage, they generally won't have the authority to sanction a discount, so they'll call their supervisor. You don't have to give any reason why you want a discount, just ask for one, don't bottle out.

To get on in life, you have to be confident - if you're not confident (which is not a failing, no one is confident all the time) you have to look confident. You have to face your fears. You have to be prepared to look like an idiot. You have to constantly challenge your own timidity. Asking for a discount is not something most people do, which is what makes you stand out. View it as some sort of consumer rite of passage.

Project X

"No one can tell me, Nobody knows, Where the wind comes from, Where the wind goes."

No one knows where they are going to end up in life. It's a mystery. Your plans and schemes will take you somewhere, but as you are not God you can't possibly know where it will take you, only that you are on a journey. That journey shapes you along the way so that you start off as one beast and end up as another. Just have the intent to make the journey.

What you should know is if you're on the wrong train, every stop is the wrong stop. The journey starts with off-loading the shit you don't want, the things that keep you a miniscule human, useless to yourself and the people you care about.

Your life is yours, not someone else's – do not put your life in another person's hands, doing that will always lead to tragedy for you. You need to be vessel worthy of the cosmic stardust which created you. Make your life your project - this is what you do when you train, why not apply it to the rest of your life? If you do this at twenty, by the time you're thirty you will have separated from the rest of the herd. But you can do this at any age because the world has changed – it is now easier to construct your own world than ever before.

TASK – Whatever you are doing, stop doing it for a week. Take a train/car/bus/helicopter/horse/bicycle to a place you have never been to before - a city, a town, or somewhere on the coast where no one knows you and you don't know them. Find six places on your country's map. List them one to six, then throw a dice – the number it shows should be the place you go to. Don't have any other considerations, just do it - stick to the place the dice has selected for you. Now you are a journey that *you* have initiated. Find cheap accommodation. Stay a few nights. Don't view your new place like a tourist, they miss everything which matters. What does it feel like being in a place where no one knows you? A place where every street you walk down is a new street? Even familiar things; shops, houses, streetlights; the pavement - look different. Take note of the postcards selling shit in the shop windows, read the local newspaper, listen to the accents, the way people speak, the different words they use. Who knows what you'll learn, but the experience will only be positive. A year at school doesn't compare.

All of life is your teacher, not your fucking school. School just spews out work zombies. When those zombies visit different areas they miss all the relevant stuff about those areas – they stopped *really* learning when they left school.

Going to a new place is a great way to discover people and how they live; and then you realise *that is you*, where you live, trapped in your bubble – going about your normal life.

Remember the dream you had where you walk out of your front door in your neighbourhood? As you walk along things start to change, your neighbourhood turns into an area you no longer recognise – you carry on but you can't find your way back? *Project X* means leaving the familiarity of your neighbourhood; going on a journey. You don't know where you'll end up, but you'll have started your journey. Unlike your dream you won't lost, because discovering the world isn't a loss, it's a gain.

Think and Grow Strong

Gang Fit says that you should create your own life, and that you should be utterly uncompromising whilst you're going about it. If you're not, you won't achieve it. People and circumstances will throw every obstacle in your way – that's par for the course. You need to have an impenetrable shield to stop it getting to you. If you've been brought up on the street or in harsh circumstances, just about everything around you wants to keep you down - so you need to be determined, resolute that you can lift yourself up and start succeeding. When good things start happening, when your first crumbs of success are realised, life starts giving you opportunities where previously there were none. Brilliant people and crazy things present themselves; they will appear out of the ether. "Why the fuck didn't I see the opportunies before?!" That's called life; you can't see things when obstacles are obstructing your vision, and you can't see things when you are looking down at the ground. Challenges will be immense, you'll have to work harder than ever before, but out of the fog you begin to see something glorious on the horizon – *your destination*.

You can ignore everything in Gang Fit, apart from this – *create your own life.* You could have a thousand lives – one you become a physicist; another, you are an entrepreneur; another, you care for animals; another, you live in the mountains – whatever. You live life on your own terms. This doesn't mean you are selfish, as a happy person is never selfish – it means nobody dominates you or stops you from creating your life.

You must know that all creation starts in your mind. *Use your mind to forge a new world.*

- PART THREE -

Now you've left the school or university gates, you can forget all that shit you learnt. So long. It was nice whilst it lasted (maybe not) but you're in a different world now. This world has a different sort of teacher and requires a different sort of knowledge. If you learnt about ox-bow lakes at school or the atomic weight of a rat's anus, you can carry that knowledge, or even expand on it, throughout your life – but do you realise how many slaves know things? They sit in their pods for forty hours a week, trapped, entombed, tied to a leash, unable to leave their front door and *turn right* because *they have to turn left*. But it's ok because they "know things".

Some people liked to be owned, they're scared of freedom. Freedom is uncertainty. Freedom is the danger of starvation. Freedom is being responsible for your own actions. So they go to work, return home, watch TV, and slowly descend into the mindless void. This void is punctuated by weekly shopping, a two-week holiday every year - and once every four years or so, the right to vote in an election to change the government - as if that makes any difference to their pathetic lives. Is Gang Fit being too harsh on the zombies? No. It's impossible to be too harsh on the fuckers. They want to infect you with their #mindvirus. Their world deserves to be smashed-up. They are trying to turn you into one of them; you should regard that as an act of war.

Who you are, what your background is, or how many gold stars you got at school – none of that matters. Some people will tell you it does, but all they are doing is trying to categorise you, put you in a box which says you have some sort of advantage, or the opposite, some sort of
disadvantage. Advice: delete these people from your life. They will only drag you down into their retarded theories and ideologies.

115

All you should be concerned with is that your life begins again tomorrow, then the next day, then the next. Too many people use their

past as an excuse for their position in life; if that's you, you need to stop that shit. It doesn't take much to do; all you need to do is take action. After a while the things which used to bring you down start to evaporate; even better, *they help you rise*, they add to your explosive power - the power to destroy the things you don't want and create the things you do want.

Gang Fit has uncovered that similarities exist between the teenager, the disaffected, the business owner, the poor, and the multimillionaire. The similarities are a desire for freedom, liberty, independence, creativity, health, and strength – being wild; not being told what to do or how to live. This is unsurprising as wildness is in our genes – we descend from hunter-gatherers who roamed the plains and slept under the stars. There is a primal force in your dna which is being suppressed by much of modern life. *You need to uncover it*. The future holds the promise of something great and transformative if you use it before it fades, and you turn to dust.

The Opportunity Generator and Amplifier

If you are intending to start a business of some sort, never forget this; *the only point of having a business is to improve your life. If your business doesn't improve your life you are in the wrong business.* You will never be told this at business school. You won't even be told this by other business owners. This is the first time you've been told it. Isn't that crazy?

Anecdote: For two years I worked Saturdays with a friend at the world-famous Portobello Road Market in Notting Hill, West London. It was a great crack. I was outdoors, and got paid cash-in-hand according to how much junk I sold to tourists. Crucially, it was only one day a week, my upper limit for employment. The person I worked with had his own business which he'd been struggling with for years. His health had suffered, his marriage was all but broken ("my wife this, my wife that"), and he was a semi-alcoholic, falling asleep in his favourite chair every night after washing down his cheese and pork pie with a bottle and a half of red wine.
One day he turned up at the market with a savage hangover, only realising in the morning that rather than drinking two bottles of red the night before, he had drunk two bottles of Port. Even though he had guzzled an ocean of vin rouge over the years, he had no taste whatsoever – a trait of all alcoholics. You could tell he was a junk drinker – he drank his wine from a half-pint glass and poured it like water from a tap. Twenty-three years in his business had turned him from a young man with a vision to an overweight fucking wreck, only a short step away from a cardiac unit. He was trapped in a nightmare, like a story from the Twilight Zone.

A few years later it eventually all went belly-up. I bumped into him – he told me he was stacking shelves in a supermarket. He was in his mid-fifties. He deserved it.

****

The future for the normal person isn't 'starting a business', self-employment, or working from home; that is not today's nature of opportunity. [Note: The idea that being employed but working from home is personal progress is misconceived – working from home is just a longer leash. People who think they're free because they work from home are like slaves who've been given a gold star by their master]

Lifestyle is your business. You should to do things which *enhance your life*. The blueprint is straightforward. You begin with an idea of the sort of life you want to live, then you add in the components which you require to live that life. At the same time you start to eliminate the shit you don't like. Kids are told at school that they should do stuff to help other people, save the planet, and other bullshit – they're told that only caring about their own lives is somehow selfish. This is complete bollocks. When a person enhances their own life they enhance the lives of people around them.

The Opportunity Generation & Amplification Machine

Fortunately, there is a resource that past generations never had, poor bastards – the Internet. The internet is the most powerful manmade creation in history. For your life you should view it is an 'Opportunity Generation & Amplification Machine'. It will help you create your new world.

The Internet: Opportunity Generator → Your Mind: Opportunity Amplifier

Your Mind: Opportunity Generator → The Internet: Opportunity Amplifier

Our brains (singularly, and as a collective) are the original 'internet' – the original opportunity generator made by Nature. And because we can't help making the universe all about us, we created the internet, the simulation of a brain.

GENERATOR: Ideas, information, serendipity, zero cost

AMPLIFICATION: Network effect, scale, connectivity

The Internet is a connectivity and information device which means that compartmentalising your life as this or that (business owner/self-employed, etc) has become irrelevant. Your life is merely an expression of how you want to live, you don't care to call yourself anything.
The internet is the Big Bang of opportunity which means there are zero (practically) costs, a trillion interconnections, and the ability to crush distance in a split second. You need no stock, no warehouse, no rent, no rates, no physical structure. You *can* have those if you want, but you are free to choose – which is the point.

You are free to decide where you live; you can have a foot in the country and one in the city. You can 'work' in the morning, as you wish, and go for a walk in the afternoon; a swim in the sea, a drink with your mates – a cream tea at small farmhouse cafeteria. You are not stuck to a desk, car, commute or any enforced schedule.

Like the Amazon Rainforest the internet is a million niches, as one agent is destroyed another is created. Tik Tok crushed Snapchat overnight (Tik Tok will eventually be crushed) – does anyone care? Of course not, *the universe was formed from creative destruction.* It's the way.

The Land of Opportunity

The greatest country (with the most opportunity) isn't the most perfect country - that's why people flock to the United States, not Finland, Norway, Switzerland, or any other country where the people only cross a completely clear road when the traffic lights signal they can. [The Definition of a Lunatic: A person who drives at 30mph on a clear open road that has a 30mph speed limit. Perfect countries are full of lunatics like this. Perfect countries have a history of taking children away from parents who they deem undesirable – they enforce their 'perfection'. This is why a free country can never ever be a perfect country].

You make your money in the Land of Opportunity and retire in the Land of Perfection. But there's a surprise ending; the US has a come up against an entity ridiculously more powerful - the Internet. [The US is powerful like the Hulk, but it's dwarfed by the internet which is like Galactus. Galactus eats planets; the internet is eating our planet]. The Internet is the new Land of Opportunity; and this land is everywhere. One day it will connect the Moon, then the Solar System, then the whole fucking Universe. It will be in the air you breathe, in the petal of every flower and in every cell of your body. Yeah, I'm repeating myself – but it's so important it *has* to be repeated. Because of the Internet, millions of clued-up unemployed people will never need a boss. You are the new Hunter-Gatherer, doing what you want, going where you want, living how you want – taking your tribe with you. Whatever you are doing you're a moron if you're not utilising the Internet. The internet is your idea on steroids.

If anyone tells you life is hard, it's true but not in the way they mean. They are stuck under a rock, scared of the real world, perpetual victims with a scarcity mindset. How to create your life is the biggest challenge you'll ever face – it's hard, but it's hard in a good way. Building a rocket ship and journeying to the stars is hard, but that's the sort of hard life you want.

Your new life is created by generating ideas and using the countless resources available to you. Incredibly, they are virtually free. Eleven years at school, and they never told you that.

2-Point Plan

This is so important that no one tells you about it at school or university.

- get rid of the shit in your life
- add in (go towards) what you want from life

Yeah, I know – Gang Fit has written about this before, but it needs to be simplified so you will *never* forget it. Whoever you are, whatever you background, whatever your skills, strengths or weaknesses, this is fundamental to creating the life you want. Nothing else comes close. Make all decisions in life with reference this. Tattoo '**2-Point Plan**' on your forearm. When you die they can engrave it on your tombstone: 'Here lies the body of someone who followed the 2-point plan'.

As time progresses people forget the reasons for being alive. Things get complicated – employment, money and 'responsibilities' start covering up what should be obvious. Further, zombies say that life is about, "helping others", "having children", "being a good person", blah, blah, all sweet and lovely - but there are millions of carers, charity workers, volunteers, parents, and nice people who are still miserable.
Follow the 2-point plan! You will feel great because you will have cut out the shit and added in what you want. This is not difficult for anyone with half-a-brain to understand. Everything good comes from it. You can be a nice person if you want; you can help others if you want – but still follow the 2-point-fucking-plan!

A fundamental prerequisite of a happy life is that it is *self-centered*. Brain-dead zombies say that being self-centered is wrong, "what a mean and horrible human being!"; they only perceive self-centered in a negative way. But all great things have come from individuals who have created something which is meaningful to *themselves*. The world's greatest buildings and gardens were created by people who followed their own ambitions. Institutions, charities, space rockets, life-saving medical procedures, wines and artisanal cheese – all the result of self-centered people. That's what Gang Fit means by self-centered.

The 2-point plan is so obvious, that people can't see it. It is so powerful, that people can't believe it. Maybe that's why it's not taught to *any* young kid at school. Yet, it's essential. Can you believe that?! An essential aspect of life not taught at school?

Repeat:

Get rid of the shit in your life. Add in what you want from life.

Gang Fit is more important than school.

Basic Leg Strength

TEST – This test you can do right now. Get into a kneeling position, like you're going to get knighted by the Queen of England. Lift your rear foot off the ground and stand up using your front leg only (do let the foot of your rear leg touch the ground whilst attempting to stand up!). Keeping both hands crossed on your chest makes the movement more difficult. Can you do it? Good – your leg strength is *acceptable*. It's hilarious watching people who can't do it, they look like they're glued to the ground. Don't be a weakling. Some people like to use the fancy Pistol Squat which is fine, but impossible if you don't have a degree of flexibility in your hamstrings.

Note: Many people mistake tightness for lack of strength, i.e., if you can't lift your straight leg out ninety degrees (parallel with the ground) in front of you it's more likely due to hamstring tightness than lack of quad/hip strength. Even if you're as strong as a fucking rhino you won't be able to do it if your hamstrings are super-tight. Yet, little-girl ballet dancers can do it. Smack any skinny moron who says you can't do it due to lack of strength.

Do this test every now and then to check how easy it is – it takes 3 seconds. If it's getting more difficult you need to do more resistance training on your legs (or you're putting on fat). If it's getting easier, all well and good. As you age it is *essential* you can still do this, as weak legs are associated with all sorts of negative physical/health conditions, as well as being a loser.

What Day is It?

I was at an all-day party - went to a shop (with others) to get more booze. Someone said, "we're at a party, it's a Thursday and no one fucking cares".

In prison they feed you, you have somewhere to sleep, everything is organized; there's routine - you go to bed and get up at the same time, you know what you'll be doing the next day, and the next, and the next. They call it a punishment yet it sounds just like a life based around full-time employment. "But I can leave my job". Yes, you can – and get another one, transferring from one prison to another. That's the slave's idea of freedom apparently.

This may seem like a stupid thing to do, but ask *any* employed person what day it is - they always know. Now ask a free person the same question - look at them, you see they have to think for a moment before they can answer? This is because the day of the week is irrelevant to them. Their connection to the world is completely different than the employed. The only time an employed zombie may lose track of what day it is, is when they're on their annual holiday. Feel sorry for them (no, don't).

A moment ago we had a 'basic leg strength test'. Now ask yourself what day of the week it is, that's your basic 'freedom test'. This isn't a joke; this is a serious test. Every free person experiences this. A slave will think you have some sort or memory or mental problem if you have difficult remembering what day it is. Quite ironic.

Gang

True story: A middle-aged overweight researcher went to an area to investigate what was going on - poking his nose into affairs which didn't concern him. A group of five men (locals) took exception to his presence so they killed him. The researcher had gone with others, including the police; they knew it was a dangerous neighbourhood. They escaped with their lives.

Where was this? A shit run-down neighbourhood? A drug infested area? No, it was the Amazon rainforest. The researcher was a 30-year expert on Amazonian tribes. The 'locals' were an isolated indigenous people – they attacked the group with bows and arrows. Someone who witnessed the incident said the tribe was usually, "a peaceful group", but "this time, there were just five armed men - a war party". Note that the tribe members had no regard for external authority or a uniform.

****

Being in a gang and having fights is closer to our ancestors hunter-gatherer lifestyle than staring at a screen in an office all day. Apparently, the former is abnormal; the latter is normal. *"Gang"* is emotively used by the media, child psychologists and other idiots for what is simply a group of friends who hang out together; a tribe, a band of brothers – nothing wrong with that. Businesses, organisations, charities, sports clubs and pop groups are all groups of individuals with a unifying element or mission, so why is a gang bad?

The idea that you should *not* be in a 'gang', is retarded. Experts say that people need social support, they say people need friends, they say people should help and support each other. What the hell does a gang do?! Yet they call it antisocial. Here's the reason why *real* gangs are hated; unlike brainwashed kids at school they live by their own rules and codes, they defend their group against outsiders, they sort out their own problems, and most of all, they don't give a shit what society thinks is right or wrong. This sounds *exactly* like a hunter-gatherer group.

Don't believe experts – being in a gang is good. Your family is a gang. Your friends are a gang. You protect them, they protect you. What benefits them benefits you, what benefits you benefits them. People want you to put the welfare of strangers over your own welfare and the welfare of your gang, don't allow it. Your welfare and the welfare of the closest people to you is the absolute fundamental of life. Hunter-gatherers knew it. The whole fucking animal kingdom knows it. The only living creatures on the planet who don't know it are the ones who heave read 200 books and went to university.

Money vs Freedom

There are 2 types of individual who trade freedom for money:

1 The employed (millions of these). They spend all their weekdays working for money. They earn money so they can pay bills and feel free at the weekend

2 The individual who is never satisfied - they want more money. The business owner/mega-rich, entrepreneur, wanker, etc. They are boring show-offs, and even more boring company; they *only* talk about making money. Men like this surround themselves with plastic women and sports cars. Women like this are childless, depressed, and drink too much wine

There are 3 types of individual who trade money for freedom:

1 The hobo/tramp/homeless/drop-out (take out the drug addict, those with mental problems). This life is tough - the heroically naïve Chris McCandless ended up dying in a bus in Alaska

2 The purposely unemployed, on welfare (gainfully or ungainfully)

3 Those who work just enough to spend the majority of time doing what they like (self-employed/part-time employee/entrepreneur/creator, etc.)

There are 4 types of individual where money vs freedom is irrelevant:

1 The individual who has investments, passive income, a business run by others, an automated income stream, etc. Anything which brings in money with minimal time involved. Money flows into their pockets whatever they are doing

2 Someone who has sold a business, made a mint (in some way), and no longer needs to work. These people may choose to spend some of their time only on projects/ideas/social enterprises which interests them – much more interesting than playing golf until they die (another form of zombiefication)

3 Professional artisans/writers who love their work. Their idea of freedom is doing their work and being paid for it. Work and freedom are the same thing

4 The landed, gentry, aristocrat; those with inherited wealth/assets; and 'rich kids'. The aristos conserve and pass on their wealth to the next generation (as is their duty), the rich kids blow it on parties, drugs – then start a fashion chain or similar, which usually fails.

****

It is far better to focus on being free (escaping entrapment) than having money. The average numbskull response, "Stupid advice. You can't be free without money!" Of course, numbskull – freedom with no money isn't freedom, it's mostly hell. Concentrating on true freedom (in today's society) necessitates being hyper-concerned with money, but not allowing money to enslave you. In fact, you have to be almost paranoid about money (but not in the way an employed person is paranoid about it) because you understand that the right sort of money (how it flows to you, how it's created) has the power to transform your life, and allow you to permanently escape the rat race.

Gang Fit chooses the freedom route over the money route but doesn't want starvation or deprivation to come with the freedom, even though it is prepared to risk those in the pursuit of freedom. First note: It may come with it for a while, but don't be a fucking weakling – being scared of having no money keeps millions of zombies at work. Second note: You won't realise that suffering is good for you whilst you're in it, *only later on when you look back on it*. It's deep, very deep – possibly the deepest part of having achieved something; that you went through immense suffering. It's possible that suffering is a *vital* part of growth. The forging of the warrior mind.

Two types of freedom (which don't involve suffering, living on nothing; i.e., *Chris McCandless Syndrome*)

- The freedom to not *have to do* anything you don't want to do

- As above, but with the additional freedom to do whatever you feel like doing, whenever you feel like doing it.

Read 'A Millionaire at $500 Per Week' later in Gang Fit about this – you'll see that anyone who is motivated and has a brain bigger than walnut can achieve the former. Why don't parents tell their kids? Why doesn't school teach it? They say that school prepares kids for life…"improves their chances" – what does that even mean? Being free (not trapped) is the best fucking thing to happen to anybody, they should be teaching that at school. Brainwashed kids have been brainwashed by adults who themselves have been brainwashed. Most teachers should be sacked. Sooner or later their work will be done by robots anyway – then they might understand how their version of education doesn't prepare anyone for real life. If schools had lessons on freedom, making money, being creative, starting a business, building a ship, making nitroglycerin, riding a horse, being wild - kids would lap it up, there'd be a reason to go to school. School is teaching young people to be employees, trading time for money…a death sentence. That's why schools are shit. A friend of mind set alight to

124

his school. Unfortunately, it didn't burn down to the ground. He was expelled. I was too young to realise he had the right idea.

The majority of people in your street are not free. You are literally surrounded by zombies; people who traded freedom (their time) for money. They are so mentally undeveloped they don't even know it. But they are not idiots in the low IQ, dribbling, retarded, butt-ugly face sort of way. Being free has nothing to do with IQ, education, knowledge, blah, blah…if it was, why is a chipmunk with its tiny fucking brain more free than your neighbour with the Mercedes? Their idiocy is far deeper than that – zombiefication infects every cell of their body.

Story: A few years back scientists discovered a parasite which lives inside the eyeballs of a certain species of fish. The *eye fluke* <u>controls</u> the fish for most of its life. When the nasty critter is ready to reproduce the host fish suddenly starts swimming closer to the surface of the water. This is because the eye flukes live inside the fish but can only reproduce inside a bird. A fish which swims closer the water surface is more likely to be eaten by a bird. Once inside the bird's gut, the eye fluke reproduces - their eggs are shed in the bird's shit, and they hatch in water. They find water snail hosts, multiply in the snails and then start searching for a host fish. They penetrate the fish's skin and work their way up to its eyeball. The fish don't know it has a parasite and it doesn't know it is being controlled. It doesn't matter if the fish has a degree in Astrophysics or a membership with Mensa, it is still being controlled by the parasite.

0.01 Per Cent

If you want to be all of these - strong, lean, fit, athletic, independent and unemployable you can't live like 99.99% of people.

Strong – 1 in 50

Strong and lean – 1 in 250

Strong, lean & fit – 1 in 500

Strong, lean, fit & athletic – 1 in 1000

Strong, lean, fit, athletic & independent/unemployable – 1 in 10,000+

As each one is added the cohort reduces in size. In a population of 100 million people only 10,000 would qualify. But the reality is they are not independent qualities - in Gang Fit's world they are connected; *they have to be connected*. Being one makes you more likely to be the other. All the qualities together should be as achievable as any one quality, even though in modern society the last category is only 1/200th as common as the first category.

What the hell is going on? If you were a wild beast you would be all of these. Humans are so intelligent they've sent rockets to Mars but so stupid they eat cornflakes for breakfast, a sandwich for lunch and pizza for supper. They're so stupid they think they can get away with eating shit and doing no exercise. They're so stupid they spend all day doing the same boring shit in the same boring place. Not you though. You are wild. And what does a wild animal want? It wants to be free; it hates being caged. A wolf will chew its leg off to escape from a trap – that's how much it fears entrapment. That's the sort of intensity you need to escape the gravitational pull of Planet Zombie.

Note: The Wild is faaar more dangerous than a zoo but no animal likes being caged. They won't trade freedom for security and the guarantee of being fed.

****

The more free you are, the less you have in common with people. If you want to be normal, go ahead, it's easy to do - you do nothing. You will be sucked in like a black hole sucks in light. But if you have any wildness, energy, individuality or sheer rage left in you which hasn't been obliterated by school and your upbringing, you cannot live like 99.99% of people. Build your body, attain dynamic health, and fight for your freedom.

A Millionaire at $500 Per Week

What keeps people trapped at work or in their business is they think they need enough money so they can have whatever they want in life – a nice house, a supercar, yacht, international travel, and other clichés. That isn't the right way to think; if you believe it, it will become the manacles around your ankles. Don't be just another fucking fool who has been taken in by the marketing of what a "good life" means.

The first and most important step into the land of your childhood dreams is to *have enough money so you <u>don't have to do anything you don't want to do</u>*.

It is far easier to do the latter than the former. If you have expensive tastes (and ambitions) the first may take $10million, the second only $500 per week. If your outgoings are low you could be free from slavery *forever* for only $300 per week.

The thing which makes people most miserable is spending their days doing stuff they don't want to do. Can you imagine that? Being born so you can spend 45 years of your life trapped in something you hate, bored out of your brain but convincing yourself it's necessary? That's retarded. You know, right? It's *not good for you* – and what's not

126

good for you is not good for the world because unhappy people make the world an unhappy place.

What's easier to make? A few hundred a week or a million? You don't need to be Einstein to work it out yet the logic seems to be lost on people who inhabit zombieland. "Oh, but I don't want to be poor all my life!" Idiot. If you have more free time because you are not doing the 9 to 5 you have more opportunity to research and start things which make you more money. *So your first aim is to be free from employment, then create your empire.* Whoever heard of a slave creating an empire?

Money should make you free - that's the whole fucking point of having it. It shouldn't make you a slave. Wanting a gold watch and a supercar before you are free means you'll be a slave forever.

Bungalow Town

- studio flat
- house
- bigger house
- bungalow
- coffin

There's a place on the English coast that I call 'bungalow town' - that's not its real name, idiot; I just call it that. I kid you not; the whole place is just bungalows. I was cycling along the coast and came across it. I didn't realise at first; "this is a pleasant place" - but it slowly dawned on me that something was wrong, like being in a horror film. The place was spotlessly clean and tidy, but no one was outside even though it was warm and the sunny. I needed to get out as I was being drawn in to its pleasantness and order – like a manicured cemetery. Fuck this - I'm not ready to die.

****

Bungalows are generally occupied by people who are one-step-from-the-grave, either because they are old or because they are boring. Old people live in bungalows because their family have left home and they downsize (they don't need the space anymore), or because increasing infirmity means stairs become a problem – they need all the rooms on one level. Boring people live in bungalows because a bungalow represents the dimming of the spark of life. [Boring people are the worst fuckers on the planet; they make you want to kill yourself. They are vampires, sucking the life-force out of you. Steer clear of them].

Every other week an ambulance arrives in Bungalow Town and quietly takes someone away, never to come back. This happens with hardly anyone noticing. The ambulance is the start of the journey from bungalow to coffin. Ashes to ashes, dust to dust, cradle to grave, don't bother putting the kettle on.

There may come a time when the idea of living in Bungalow Town becomes appealing to you. You have to fight it. Smash your head against a brick wall, run as fast as you can until you almost pass out, walk inches from the edge of a steep cliff, stare into the eyes of a 150lb Rotweiler - do something, *anything*, which knocks the shit out of slowly dying *(see next essay)*. Your next move after downsizing to a bungalow is downsizing to a coffin – no fucker ever *upsizes* from a bungalow; it's like they are trapped in a hell which they don't know is hell. That's the worst form of hell, one which infects your mind, unaware that the underbelly of 'pleasant' bungalow town is eternal nothingness, tiny herbaceous borders, and the antiseptic silence of God's waiting room.

Knock the Shit Out of Slowly Dying

Nobody heard him, the dead man,
But still he lay moaning:
I was much further out than you thought
And not waving but drowning.

Poor chap, he always loved larking
And now he's dead
It must have been too cold for him his heart gave way,
They said.

Oh, no no no, it was too cold always
(Still the dead one lay moaning)
I was much too far out all my life
And not waving but drowning.

'Not Waving but Drowning' – Stevie Smith, 1957

Stevie Smith tried to commit suicide when she was only eight years old - can you imagine that? Poor cow.

Maybe not her but the majority of people are depressed because their lives are boring as shit. They're going nowhere. The thing about going nowhere is that it actually feels like you are slowly sinking. Drowning. It's not that people can't cope with too much (being busy), they can't cope with nothing. *Nothing* slowly kills more people than being

128

busy. Modern day depression comes from the purposeless *void*, not from being overworked.

****

Some people are so bored with their lives they fill it up with full-time employment. Can you believe that?! That gives them something to do, but it's not the answer, it makes things worse - it makes their brains shrink to the size of a peanut. Not only do they stay bored but they become boring – spouting shit about their jobs.

The reality is that you are a nobody. Even the most famous person in the world is still a nobody. Apart from your family and closest friends, no one gives a shit about you. Don't worry, it's not personal, they've got their own lives and irrelevant problems.

There is nothing wrong with being a nobody, but there is everything wrong with being bored, and being a bore. If you are bored with your life you need to knock the shit out of slowly dying. You need to fill the void. You can do this through art, through nature, through religion, through a dedication, through the oceanic, or through rioting and smashing a place up. The motivation is the same – feeling alive. When you are bored you feel like a nobody. When you are excited, doing interesting shit and creating something, *you are still a nobody* but you *feel* like a somebody.

What slowly dying looks like:

Physical – getting fat, feeling tired all the time, <u>having no energy</u>

Psychological – being sensible, following a boring routine, supporting Arsenal football club, <u>having no energy</u>

If you're young, this shouldn't be happening to you – if it is, God help you; you are already becoming like the zombies and old farts around you. You need to escape that shit or you'll end up in Zombie Town, or worse, Bungalow Town

Knock the shit out of slowly dying. How do you do that? Wait a minute…

Flat surfaces

The older you get the flatter your life becomes. The flatter your life becomes the older you get.
Climbing trees, jumping over walls, physical challenges, running up stairs, doing dangerous things, running from the cops, having fights, cycling superfast down a hill, random shit – what do all these have in common?

129

- They improve your brain
- Adults hardly do them

Studies have found that climbing a tree improves your brain; not only that, it improves your brain instantly. This must be why so many adults are idiots, they stopped climbing trees. In fact, they stopped doing all sorts of things which improves their brains. They evened out their lives – flat surfaces (pavements, offices, factory floors); flat lives (9-5 employment, routine, financial stability, regular meals, central heating) and flat activities like long distance running and watching F1.

All the things you did as a kid improves your brain. Most of the things you do as an adult deadens your brain.

Being young is variability; getting old and being sensible is petrification, taking out unevenness reducing risk and uncertainty; never doing anything physically challenging. No hits of adrenaline, never jumping off high walls, never doing anything frightening – never doing any shit which makes your heart beat with excitement or fear. The problem is that the complete absence of variation is death. The zombies are choosing death over life. Who told you that is being sensible? Kill them.

CHALLENGE – retain or reintroduce variation. Physical, psychological and emotional. Ask a person out for a date, do something risky, start a fight (against someone who deserves it), face fear, learn to juggle, leave your job. Move to a mountainous area, do terrifying shit. Quit your job, gatecrash a nightclub or party, swim down a river, motorcycle across a desert, hang glide, fight crocodiles, spend 48hrs with a homeless person, use public transport without paying, take a week off work without asking, make a million dollars – you get the idea.

In other words…the way *to knock the shit of slowly dying* is to stop being a sensible wanker – do 'stupid' stuff. You're welcome.

Snakes and Ladders

You ever played the game snakes and ladders? You throw a dice (fuck off, "die") and attempt to get from square one (start) to square one-hundred (finish) before your opponent. If you land on a square with the bottom of a ladder you go up; with the head of a snake, you go down. In the final straight, when you're practically home and dry, there's the head of a snake; it's the longest snake on the board - if you throw the wrong number and land on *that* square you slide down the snake almost to the beginning. Why would they do that? They're sadists.

It's because it emulates real life. One day you're cock-of-the-walk, master-of-the-universe, blah, blah – the next day you're on your arse because you've been given a kicking by real-life. It's great to feel self-pride and be happy with your achievements, but the moment you become careless, arrogant, and start acting like a prick on a power-trip, that's when the snake is going to appear.

Whoever invented the game Snakes & Ladders, knew about life. Apparently, the game originated in ancient India, like 20 million years ago, where it was known as 'Mokshapat' or 'Moksha Patumu'. The squares in which ladders start were supposed to stand for virtue, and those with the head of a snake, for evil. This is timeless wisdom; you cannot escape it. Don't be a dummy.

Paid Employment

Paid employment is unnatural - that's why so many people hate it. Work for free.

The problem with employed people is they expect to be paid for their work, and don't expect to be paid for their leisure. This is what keeps them trapped. You should divorce time and money in that you may have to put in a ton of work with no guarantee of pay, but equally not have a problem with being paid for 'no work'.

If you hate employment:

Switch off your brain at work; switch on during 'leisure'.

What the zombie does:

Switches on brain at work; switches off during leisure.

Freedom means never *having to* get out of bed for a wage. You are only going to achieve that if you start using your leisure time to *create something* rather than for mindless entertainment. The pressure from your friends, partner, or other zombies may be to take it easy, go out, "watch a movie", go shopping, or do some shit which fills the weekend. Keeping the company of these people is like trying to run in treacle. They are holding you back (whether they know it or not). Kill the fuckers. The company you keep is the most important thing which determines how well you'll do in life. If your friends are mindless morons, it is better having no company.

'Work for free, get paid for leisure' - the reverse of most people's mindset. In fact, they would regard this statement as ludicrous. That's because they don't have the capacity to understand something outside their experience. Once you understand the reason why a gardener creates a beautiful garden you start to shift your mindset about being able to profit from leisure.

Being paid per hour is bullshit. Being paid *forever* because you enjoy what you do is freedom.

Death Ground Strategy

The Death Ground Strategy *guarantees* you can leave your shit job, but you may become homeless, starve, or even die if you can't find an alternative way to make an income (or some scheme) to help you survive. The Sensible Strategy is to save money, have some investments or start something on the side which makes extra money whilst you're employed. The downside is this may take ten years or *never happen*, as life, the job itself, or other commitments get in the way. You stay trapped, get fat, and your brain turns into something resembling porridge. Most people choose the Sensible Strategy as it *is* the sensible route. They're sensible people.

1 If you want money more than you hate employment, you can choose the sensible strategy.
2 If you hate employment more than you want or love money, you can use the death ground strategy.
3 If you are lazy + spineless you can buy lottery tickets (stop reading this book, you don't deserve it)

If you use the death ground strategy (you have no safety net) your normal life will explode. The explosion will temporarily wipe out what is bad *and* good in your life. If you utilise the sensible strategy you should listen to the internet experts on how to make money, but understand that the probability of leaving employment forever will be less than 20%.

Generally, life should be a series of 'Safe to Fail Experiments' i.e., if something doesn't work out it's not a calamity – you survive unscathed. That's all well and good, but the reality is that some things are so important that you risk complete destruction for your beliefs. The danger of the death ground approach is also its superpower, you have zero options but to survive. The problem for most people is that having a wage blunts their focus, whereas facing starvation engages parts of you, good or bad, you didn't know existed.

Normal people do everything they can to avoid it, but the reality of the Universe, and everything in it, is creation from destruction. What is the problem with destroying your current life? If it's pissing you off, fucking destroy it.

Death Ground Strategy

- Cast iron guarantee you escape shit employment
- No guarantee you won't end up penniless and homeless
- Your focus will be sharpened – 'sink or swim' effect
- Desperation overcomes timidity/fear. You take on challenges you would normally avoid
- You engage personal qualities and resources (good *and* bad) you didn't know existed
- Over time you get used to pressure which crushes the normal person
- You have more free time to research and pursue opportunities
- You won't have the money to pursue some opportunities

Sensible Strategy

- No guarantee you will ever escape employment
- You'll be able to pay your bills
- If you have a family, they won't be put in jeopardy
- You will never face real hardship
- Your friends (or people you meet) won't think you're a loser
- A regular wage will dull your ambitions
- Your savings may disappear very quickly on leaving employment, forcing you to return to work
- The 'sensible strategy' is really a form of self-bullshitting - you are all talk, no action; just another wage slave

If you have understood the message of Gang Fit, there is only one answer. When you are in a shit low-paid job you will never save enough money (or buy enough assets) to be able to leave employment. If you're from a poor background and have little access to money you should ignore advice from people who have always been comfortable, *until you are comfortable.* They have no concept of what it is like in your situation. They are half-people, psychologically undeveloped. They are telling you to grow crops and wait whilst you are starving to death. Their advice to you is useless in your position.

The thing you should develop, and rely on, is your warrior mind, bomb-proof determination, and the absolute fucking refusal to give up. The Death Ground Strategy will force this upon you. It's merciless, it's fearsome – most people would never do it.

Being Scared

Blind rage overcomes fear

Desperation overcomes fear

Saving a child's life overcomes fear

When you've got a reason big enough you overcome fear. Hating being trapped at work so much so that life is an utter fucking misery, means you need to leave employment to save your life. It's that or your soul dies.

Leave shit employment forever. The day you quit your job will feel like pure freedom. Enjoy the initial feeling (it will soon turn to dread), then get to work as if your life depended on it.

You are not a Collective

People want to put you in a box, label you, say you are *this* or *that* – don't stand for it. Some people say that people "like you" have good qualities; others say that "your type" have bad qualities – ignore both sides, they are wankers. They obliterate who you are; you're just an object, not an independent person. To them you're a stereotype. Their labels for you promote the idea that you are an unsentient part of a collective, you can't think for yourself, you don't have your own mind, your own thoughts, your own brain, your own aspirations, your own strengths and weaknesses – you are a clone.

A person who looks like you or has a similar background is not your representative or spokesperson – they don't speak for you. Leave any group which demands your conformity; what they're really after is power – don't fucking give it to them. They won't control you - you can't be controlled.

****

Be proud of who you are but don't get bogged down in your past – that's how wars start. All around the world wars are started and caused by fuckers who are part of a tribe, culture, or ethnic group – carrying on their pathetic gripes over the generations; squabbling about some shit that happened 500 years ago. These pinheads get born, fight, then die – like programmed robots. Don't waste your time arguing about all the wrongs that people like you suffered centuries ago – they're all dead. You are no different to the people who wronged you.

The only war you should be waging is the one against zombiefication.

Zombies label you. They want you to fight their wars. When you refuse, you are "letting the side down". Then they'll start to denigrate you, then hate you. All the world hates an apostate. An apostate is someone who has left the clan. The clan detest the apostate

134

more than their enemy. Don't worry, pea-brains hate independent people, it's in their nature. Stay strong, stand firm, and resist their bullets and bombs with your will-power. They will go to their graves as slaves, you will go to yours as a sovereign individual.

Two mini-essays on **action**. If you have a problem with repetition, understand that Gang Fit can do anything it likes:

The World's Favourite Hobby

If you want to write a book, write a book. If you want to build muscle, build muscle. If you want to lose weight. Lose weight. If you want to make money, make money. Some (many) fuckers will tell you it's not that simple - there's not enough time; there are too many problems, blah, blah…

What's the world's favourite hobby? Making excuses. Loads of excuses, a shit-tonne of excuses. Excuses vomit out of people the way promises vomit out of politicians. Take note of how the average zombie talks. You'll notice how many bullshit reasons they spew for why they can't do this or that. These are the sort who are going to change something major next week, next month, next year – you've heard that right? There are 100 reasons why you can't do something, 101 of them are bullshit. People who make excuses are fucking irritating, tell them to their faces they're bullshitters – then look in the mirror and say it to yourself

Action Beats Bullshit

When you walk in a straight line, depending on your ambition you are either getting further or getting closer to your starting point. Either way the distance behind you is growing and the distance in front of you is reducing.

TASK – Whatever you're thinking of doing, just start it. Do you know how many people say, "I'm going to write a book", "I'm going to get fit", "I'm going to be a millionaire"? Millions of them. And what happens? Nothing. Nothing happens. Stop talking bullshit about doing this or that. Stop reading books about doing this or that. Stop taking advice about this or that. Stop sitting under a tree in a park, thinking about this or that. Somehow people convince themselves that all of that shit means they are being proactive. That's delusion. All the 'action' is in their heads.

Young people have all sorts of ambitions and visions of a life in their heads – if that's you, act on those visions before you get old. Chronic inaction is like slowly bleeding to death. It's the worse form of death there is – a complete waste of a life.

The Downside of Losing Money is All in Your Head

Going from $100 per week to $500p/wk feels great. Going from $500 to $1k feels great, but going back to $500p/wk feels miserable. Going from $1k to $2k feels great, but falling back to $1k p/w feels rubbish. Going from $2k to $5k feels great, but sliding back to $2kp/wk feels crap. At what level does this stop? If a person wants a fortune it's the right attitude to have, never being satisfied - but it's not healthy. If all you want from life is lots of money you don't have a life. Always wanting more money is a sort of illness. If being *comfortable and free* doesn't make you happy, being *more comfortable* won't make you happy. Your problem isn't lack of comfort but that you are ungrateful. In your rise to the top don't turn into a prick.

TEST: If you lose money when you're wealthy, turn this ungrateful dynamic on its head by giving some of your remaining money away. This will defeat your demons.

Hell is You

If you don't do anything in life, your time on earth will slowly turn to shit. Your existence will become so meaningless that a short bus ride to your local shops will be the highlight of your day; you might as well kill yourself. You'll be no good to yourself or anyone else – you could exit the gene pool and no one would notice. That's sad. But many sad people still have someone who loves them, someone who cares about their happiness and wellbeing. If this is you, you need to honour that person by not destroying your life through fear, timidity, ignorance, blaming others, laziness, and chronic inaction. The thing about improving your life is that you also improve the lives of the people who care about you. If you hate yourself, think about the people who *really* support you and the effect your disintegrating, unfulfilling, shit life is having on them. Stop feeling sorry for yourself. Stop sitting in your bedroom with the curtains drawn, listening to miserable songs produced by people who only want to make money from self-absorbed non-entities like you. If you've dyed your hair green, put on weight, and walk at one-mile an hour, something seriously needs to change. You need to save yourself. If you can't do it for yourself, do it for the people who care about you.

Make the World More Unequal

Your aim in life should be to diverge from the zombies; you don't want equality, you don't want to be the same, you don't want to have what everyone else has. Real diversity has fuck all to do with skin colour, gender, or some other vomit people talk about. Zombiefication overwhelms all that pseudo diversity shit. De-zombiefication is the real diversity, not what type of car you own, the house you live in or the colour of your socks. People talk about diversity but bleat about lack of equality, what sort of stupidity is that?

Don't get caught up in other people's notions of how the world should be. Real diversity is the magic of life – *make more of it* by separating yourself from the homogenous mass. Look at health, fitness, and strength – why would you want to be equal to others? They're pathetic. Free yourself from the aspirations of others, they're not interested in diversity, they're only trying to make everyone think the same; the opposite of diversity. The real diversity is diversity of thought and diversity of living how you want to live. Make the world more unequal by choosing how to spend your time. When they're at work, you're swimming in a lake. When they are rioting, you're climbing a mountain. When they are voting, you're crossing a desert. When they are consuming you are creating. When they are complaining, you are planning. When they are comfortable, *you* are rioting. Fuck them. Live how you want.

Like Attracts

If your friends are idiots, you're an idiot. If your friends are fat, you are fat. If they are poor, you are poor. If they are ugly, you are ugly. If they are losers, you're a loser. If they are weak, you are weak. If they are wankers, you're a wanker.

When you look at your friends, you look at yourself. When you start improving in life, the quality of your friends improves.

TASK - Before your life starts improving you should drop low quality friends. Better to have no friends than bad friends. This in itself improves your life. You owe them nothing. Keeping hold of bad friends is a sign that you are fucking about – you are not serious about progressing. Whether you drop them one by one or all at the same time is up to you – either way, you have to see less and less of them. Eventually you'll wonder why they were friends in the first place. If you do bump into them later in life, they will look the same, talk the same, and discuss shit that is of no interest to you. Well done, you've moved on.

A Job Kills Your Dreams

Going to work every day blocks out why your life is going nowhere. It's an avoidance strategy. It lets you ignore hard questions. This is why a dose of unemployment (through redundancy/walking-out/banging the boss's daughter), or being forced to live in a cave for 30 days (an experiment) is positive for people who don't have a walnut for a brain.

Being trapped in employment kills your dreams but pays your bills.

How your dreams are killed:

1 A regular wage reduces your drive – you're 'comfortable'
2 Working 35hrs a week reduces your free time
3 The people you work with have a slavery mindset which infects you
4 Like a long prison sentence you become institutionalised
5 A good job is seen as success; there's no need to try
6 The longer you're employed the more fearful you become of unemployment
7 You lose faith in your own ability to make money

Let's reverse the idea that the employed are in a better position than the unemployed. The employed have money - a car, house (perhaps), two children, a cat, and a membership to a fancy gym with tennis courts and a juice bar. Compared to them you are a loser – you have no money, you shop at cheap supermarkets, you live in shit-town, and the heels of your shoes are worn down at an angle.

Note: Only a few rich people (who don't give a damn) or the poor have shoes worn down heels. The rich may choose to look poor, but the truly poor don't have the choice not to look poor. If you have little cash, you know it right? Some stupid comfortable people talk shit about how buying one expensive item is better and lasts longer than a few cheap items – what these idiots don't understand is that a poor person never has enough money to buy an expensive item. Proof that people who have always been comfortable are the dumbest individuals on the planet. Further, if you get into a fight or need to scramble over a high wall to escape a gang or the cops, is it better to be wearing something cheap or Louis Vuitton trousers and Gucci loafers?

Back to the point: If you have no job, you may have less money than an employed person but your potential is greater, you are not tied down. You have no boss telling you what to do. The day is yours; you can try what you like. Think about it this way - is it better to be free or a comfortable slave? Having no money is only a temporary problem whereas being a wage-slave is a chronic condition. Pity the employee – getting drunk on a friday night after work is medication for their chronic condition.

Being unemployed means you may look like a loser to others, but if you are *gainfully unemployed* i.e., developing your talents, researching, experimenting and building your future, you will one-day leave them behind - the poor zombies won't realise what happened, they'll still be stuck in slavery but you'll be free.

****

Employment kills your dreams; unemployment fuels your dreams. Some people who have lost their jobs because of some circumstance have been given the biggest opportunity of their lives. Years later they will look back to it as the best thing that ever happened to them.

Unemployment scares the shit out some people but liberates others. The ones who are scared will desperately scramble back to work even accepting worse conditions than their previous job. If you have any self-pride you will never accept that – rather starve. You can feel sorry for the employed, but don't mix with them – they may infect you with their mind-virus.

****

If you are young and ambitious a job should only ever be temporary. A job is like cancer, it weakens you. Staying too long will severely inhibit your progress. Families actually have parties when their kids pass their driving test, gets a job or a promotion. The zombies are actually celebrating being trapped and conforming. Yet when their kids were young they praised them for drawing a picture or singing a song – what the hell happened? Even parents can't be trusted!

If you've been writing, painting, fighting, creating or producing for six years but make no money from it - people think you're a loser. The next two years when you make good money from it - people think you're a winner. Don't expect people to understand or support your efforts if you are making no money from it, but ignore their bullshit praise when you make something of yourself from it. Their opinions are worthless.

It doesn't matter about your worn-out shoes or your lack of money, all that matters is where you're heading. Just keep going, don't stop. Only stop when you're dead.

Monster

The real enemy isn't the one you can see, but the one who looks normal. You don't know they're the enemy until you step out of line. There are millions of people like this, they're everywhere. Scratching their surface reveals a monster. What makes the monster really terrifying is they think they are being reasonable. The reasonable person will oppress you, take away your freedom to speak, imprison you, and watch you slowly die because they believe you are being unreasonable – you either don't believe what they believe or you simply question it. Your individuality is at odds with their reasonableness.

Don't be scared of the dictator, the dictator creates resistance, people fight back – you'll have allies. But you should be very scared of the normal person, they don't create resistance because their views are the zeitgeist; only a troublemaker or uninformed idiot would disagree with their reasonable views. The monster will take away your rights because your views are faulty. You need to be re-educated before you can participate in normal society where normal and reasonable people live.

When you start thinking for yourself you instantly become a threat to normal people, they can see you don't give a shit about their lives and their beliefs. They think you're the monster, which is laughable as you have no interest in controlling people or telling *them* how *they* should live. If you are young and wild you need to protect your freedom. Leave other people alone, but if they try to control or dominate you, fight like a fucking tiger. They can't control you.

As you progress you will meet other people like you, not because they look like you but they think like you – individuals of all colours and races who value freedom over slavery. The don't give a damn about the zeitgeist or what society expects - just like you. All they care about is creating something, improving their lives and the lives of their tribe. This may be in art, sport, business, farming – whatever, it doesn't matter. Some may be rich, some may be poor – they've rejected the rat race, conformity and living like a trapped zombie. Just like you.

****

The real enemy is your next-door neighbour. Beneath the surface of millions of normal looking people is a monster. A 'reasonable' monster. A monster who knows what's good for you.

Major and Minor Keys

Major: You, your family, the people you love

Minor: Everybody else

Do-gooders and other weirdos want you to spend more time concerned with the plight of others than yourself. Stuff that. All the people who need your help don't give a fuck about you, why should they? Return the favour. The real point is not that you should be a prick and not help *anybody*, but that you should ignore people who think you should care about what they care about.

Gang Fit will annoy many people as they think its message is anti-social, as if looking after yourself and your family isn't something that humans haven't been doing forever, fucking idiots. Humans were never evolved to be concerned about other people outside their extended family and band of brothers/sisters. Arsenal fans, depressed people, poor people, minorities, ugly people, fat people – they all need help; let other people help them.

Nettles

Have you ever been stung by a nettle? Most people have heard that a dock leaf (*Rumex obtusifolius*) alleviates the sting from a nettle (*Urtica dioica*), but what they don't know is the pain from the sting is soothed by the crushed nettle leaf itself (try it out). The nettle provides the cure for its own sting. What sort of bullshit is that?! Seems sadistic to hurt you than relieve you – if that was a person they wouldn't be right in the head. However, the natural world is very intelligent, it does things for a good reason.

****

If you have a problem, maybe the answer to the problem is hidden in the problem itself? This could be totally wrong, in which case burn this book to alleviate your irritation.

Surviving Shit Street

If you live in a shit area, have you seen the guys with headphones on dancing and swinging their arms around? You think they're happy? Shit no, far from it - they are singing and dancing on their own graves. A grave with a headstone which reads, "Here lies the dead hopes and dreams of a young person". They are not having a good time – they are either mentally unstable or are doing it as a reaction to the shit of their everyday lives. It's a coping mechanism. They exaggerate happy emotions because their lives are nothing. Gang fit says this because it knows all the shit they don't teach at school.

If you live in shit street for too long it will start to affect your mind – all in bad ways. Eventually, the irresistible force of shit street will completely overwhelm you – too much trouble, too much tragedy, too many friends' dead, too many scars. Everything

141

has its limit. You have a limit which shit street *will* overwhelm. The lessons you learn
a
nd the toughness you gain from living in a shit area should allow you to move *out of that area*. If it doesn't, what the fuck are you doing?

Some places are so bad, the only way to survive is to leave.

No matter what Gang Fit has told you about getting strong, being street smart, building your physical and psychological armoury, the only long-term way to survive the street is to escape the street – no one who stays in the street for life, survives it. The advantages you get from living in shit street will only allow you to thrive in shit street for so long. Look at the long-term residents of shit street, their faces are etched with the bullshit of living in an area where you open your front door to garbage, filth, cracked pavements and brain-dead zombies.

If you live in shit street and have a shit job (90% of jobs are shit) you have problems squared. However, if you have a brain you have been given a gift, the gift of sheer hatred of your existence, like a simmering nuclear bomb – this will give you the energy to escape.

Question: If the area you live in is crap what's better for you - changing your 'internal perceptions' or changing where you live? Meditation gurus, mindset experts and people who tell you to find 'inner calm' say the world is what it is, neither positive nor negative, it's how you perceive it that matters. That's pure vomit. The people who say that are comfortably rich or comfortably retarded. If you live in a shit area and have a shit life; you have to *escape it*, not realign your freakin' chakras (whatever). Going for a walk in the woods is far better; it calms your mind and you are physically out of shit street. Take any positives out of your situation, yes. Use coping mechanisms to survive, yes. Your mind works for you or against you, yes. But if you are smothered in shit, you get out of that fucking shit as soon as you can. You need to survive before you can escape, but don't cope so well that you don't ever change your situation – millions of zombies do that shit; coping with an unsatisfying job, relationship or rubbish financial situation. Coping is necessary sometimes but the best way to 'cope' is to leave that shit behind. Some people are so stupid they use meditation apps on their phones. Sure, that will make their miserable lives better.

Life Saving Advice - If you have been living in a shit area for years, you *have to leave*. If you never leave, everything good about you will die.

Expectations, Reframing, Mindset, Blah, Blah…

You can like two things, but when you expect one *and get the other*, that other thing (which you normally like) can become disgusting. In other words, your expectations change how you view things.

TEST – This is a simple test, but you have to find the right person to use as your guinea pig. Find someone you know who likes coffee *and* red wine. When they are relaxing, watching some shit on TV, ask them if they'd like a coffee. If so, go to the kitchen and warm up some red wine and put it in a cup (like a cup of coffee) – take it to them and say there was no milk so you made them a black coffee (at a glance, red wine in a mug looks like black coffee). Sit down and wait to see what happens. It's hilarious. On taking the first sip of 'coffee' they will be disgusted by the taste, practically spitting it out. They thought they were getting coffee but instead got a mouthful of red wine. Even though they like red wine, their expectation that the drink was coffee meant the red wine tasted like skunk's piss. This works every time – try it out on different people.

In eleven years at school did you ever do a test like this? Of course you fucking didn't, because it's a test which highlights something important, it makes you think (as well as being funny) and the object of school isn't to make you think but to make you copy and learn 'facts'. A book could be written about the implications of this test alone – yet school never taught you?! Fuck school.

Lesson: Depending on your mindset what you normally like can become disgusting, and the reverse, what you hate can become something you like. The person you most love can become the person you most hate. Finding a dead mouse in your favourite food can put you off that food forever. If you are starving to death you will eat food from bins, the pavement, or half eaten by strangers – you may even eat someone's vomit. Ok, it's not that you would like eating someone's vomit (what's wrong with you?) just that you would do it to survive.

How you react to things, how you perceive things, how you think about things is what matters – you can make life work for you or work against you. People are scared of spiders, heights, birds and other things which other people take in their stride. People love food which turns them fat and causes disease. All this can be overturned. If you have negative views or reactions to things, that's quite usual – but if your preconceived notions are holding you back, you can change your beliefs about them in an instant. It doesn't take years of therapy and 'relearning'; you can change things in a second. If you have addictions or vices which are doing you no favours, you can drop them faster than a heavyweight knockout, even if they've been a habit for years.

Look at the old fossils who say, "I know what I like and what I don't like" – they go about their stupid routines and the same way of doing things, never trying something different. Most people are not self-aware. If you want to progress you need to become self-aware, aware of your limitations, aware that many of your beliefs have no real basis. People live and die not having a clue they were wankers – their opinions, likes and dislikes based on bullshit.

What you think you like, can be changed. What you think you are scared of, can be changed. Who you think you are, can be changed. What you think you can achieve, can be changed. All of it comes from your mind. It sounds like psychobabble bullshit, but it's true. Steer clear of people who say, "a leopard doesn't change its spots" or "you can't teach an old dog new tricks"; they are not the sort of people you need in your life. They think they know you; but they know shit - they don't know you. They are putting you down, scoffing at your ambitions. Delete them.

How you view things can destroy your life or make your life. Don't be like the losers who are stuck in their ways. You've found out from this test that the mind has the crazy power to turn your likes and dislikes upside down in a instant. Even if you never do the test, some situation or event in your life may demolish what you thought you believed in a second.

90% 'Correct' but 100% Dead

Here's an example of normal school stupidity; in an exam you get points for showing how you worked out a maths problem even if the final answer is incorrect. Amazingly, if you get the answer right but don't show the working out you get points deducted. What sort of arse-banditry is that? If you're a free-runner and you 'calculate' that you can jump from one building to another but you fall to your death instead, what points do you get? If you start a business and have a perfect looking business plan with all the right elements, projections, market conditions, blah, blah, but your business fails after one year owing a shit-tonne of money, what points do you get?

Ok, you could argue that doing ninety-nine things correct and only one thing wrong means you deserve some credit, and that all you need to do is change one thing – you are closer to your goal. That means nothing in real life. Only results matter. Check it out when do important work for someone which you get wrong; "oh, I got most of it right!" What do you think they will say? Will they give you any points? Fuck it they will.

Real environments are constantly changing, what may work one day may not work another, and the reverse, what didn't work for years may one day work because the environment has changed. You've done nothing different but the outcome has changed. Older athletes know that the training that works for them at 35 isn't the same training that worked for them at 21.

It's good to try things out and experiment. If your efforts fail you get feedback i.e., experience – there is nothing wrong with that. But the idea that life will credit you with some sort of external reward for messing up is only something you learn from dumb teachers at school.

School, Life, and Zombies

In real life you can make shit up, cheat, copy, get help with passing tests, set your own deadlines, decide what you want to learn, drop shit you don't like, and go to the toilet without having to ask for permission. School is so unlike real life that it's practically the reverse. Rather, school is unlike what *your life should look like*. If your life is like school, you don't have a life. You don't have any power. You have one hundred masters. Welcome to the world of the majority of people, scuttling around like ants – is that what you want? The message of Gang Fit (if you hadn't already realised) is not to take advice from the average person. The average person is born, goes to school, goes to work, then dies. "Oh, you hate normal working people. How disgusting. Who do you think you are?!" Shut up, zombie. Stick to your dull life of being sensible, moderation, and eating a balanced low-fat diet. Your life is a living death to people who value freedom. The life of a free independent person pisses you off because they don't give a shit what you believe.

****

Normal people will either love you or hate you; love you because you are what they want to be; hate you because you have what they can't have. If you want to be a normal person, go to school, become employed and *stay employed* – congratulations, you've become a zombie.

Same Shit, Different Day

To be a normal person (zombie) you have get used to the idea of the same routine for 1000 years. That's what it will feel up. It's a non-prison life sentence. Even if you have different jobs it is still the same boring shit. Get up, go to work, go home, watch tv, have a wank, go to sleep – visit friends at the weekend. Gang Fit has it on good authority that it's better being dead. School is preparing kids for this – worse, it is *grooming* them for it, so the school day replicates the work day; 8 hours a day, 5 days a week and a gold star for good behaviour.

The most boring people to be around are state school teachers – listen to them talk; academia, tests, lessons, exams and useless BS – none of them talk about making money, none of them talk about building a physique, none of them talk about starting a business; none of them have any idea that life outside the school gates is nothing like school. They've educated themselves to stupidity – the special sort of stupidity that only the educated have. This is why teachers tend to socialise together, no one with a brain can tolerate their company. These idiots have been given eleven years influence over kids. Can you imagine that? "Give me the child, I'll give you the man". No wonder so many adults are vacant.

The *same shit everyday* will be your life unless you do something about it. Fight it. Don't allow it to happen. Delete the people from your life who are trying to get you to accept it, trying to brainwash you. They want to change you from an independent wild creature into a brain-dead zoo animal. The funny thing is, they're not even happy – they're sick, they're overweight, they're on medication, and they don't have enough money. Yet they are telling you how to make your life? Fuck them. Fuck school. Fuck teachers. Fuck zombiefication. If you think that is too extreme, you haven't yet realised how dangerous normal people are.

Escape Hardship, Then Escape Comfort

Escaping from comfort is more difficult than escaping from hardship. Escaping from hardship only involves money whereas comfort is an insidious systemic condition - it smothers you; wraps itself around you like a snake. Hardship feels bad, it's obvious you don't want it – it creates the desire to escape from it. Comfort feels good; why would anyone want to stop doing something which feels good? That's its power.

The most destructive things in life aren't the things which feel bad but the things which feel good. Comfort feels sooooo good.

Two things happen when you become too comfortable; 1/ you get physically soft; 2/ you start talking shit. Progress comes from discomfort, not comfort – there is no way you can improve in *anything* if you are comfortable. Always being physically and psychologically comfortable turns you into a marshmallow.

Once you have left hardship (congratulations) and achieved comfort, *you have to reintroduce hardship* – physical hard work, business or creative challenges, new horizons to be investigated. The world is full of comfortable poor people and comfortable rich people – that's why half the world is overweight and fucking ill; addicted to shit food, shit entertainment and 'labour saving' devices. When these people get old they can hardly walk up a flight of stairs. They deserve it.

146

A Gang Fit individual isn't like the masses, they don't give a damn what other people think is important - what others think is important is bullshit. They fight against entrapment, being controlled or being told what to do. When the world wants to give or sell them comfort, they go towards hardship. They understand that comfort is a cage.

Fat Boy Get Lean

Gang Fit isn't a diet book – diet books are wank. If you live as a wild, free, independent SOB you should never need a diet book. Being overweight is for domesticated people, office workers and the "I'm-so-depressed-I-can't-stop-eating-junk-until-I've-sorted-out-my-emotions", idiot. Cookery books are the number one bestseller, followed by diet books. In a world where a billion people are still starving that's bullshit. People are like pigeons trapped in a room with an open window, they haven't got the basic commonsense to escape. If you've done all the tests, tasks and challenges in Gang Fit it's unlikely that you're overweight, it's not your mindset – but if you have still have some blub you need to sort it out. But Gang Fit still isn't a diet book…

****

There's nothing worse looking than a flabby out of shape waist. If you have *any* self-respect you shouldn't allow it. But first, let's get something straight - you see those lard-arse sumo wrestlers? They've got even more fat than your mother in-law with the bingo-wings but they *have a six-pack*, it's just covered with mounds of blubber, that's what's required for their sport, no shame in that. Sumos are tremendously strong and do all sorts of exercises, they have tremendously well-developed abdominal muscles. It used to be the case that post-career they'd lose all their weight and look normal – less so now because loads of non-Japanese do it. [The Japs are unlike any other population in the world, they have a culture of discipline and respect – so much so, that they can't understand people who don't think like them. This is why they have the capacity to be murderously dangerous to outsiders. The underbelly of the 'perfect society' is complete intolerance to anyone who is different].

You have a six-pack you only need to reveal what is already there. So, it's not about "getting a six-pack" but getting leaner. Once you're lean your midsection will look fine as it is. Your midsection may look different to someone else's – doesn't matter, you're lean. You don't need to do loads of specific waist exercises like a gym moron, but you do need to do some form of resistance exercise (not necessarily in a gym) as that builds muscle, makes you heroic, and is good for your health.

Never Jog

147

It's easy to lose fat. People who can't shift the blubber are not only mentally weak, they are doing the wrong thing. When they *keep doing the wrong thing* they are mentally stupid as well as mentally weak - the hallmark of the person who has been fat for years but "wants to lose weight".

Don't believe the stuff about being genetically fat, leave that to the deluded. It *may* be that you have a predisposition to put on fat but that is meaningless; what you eat and how you live is the deciding factor. There were no 'genetically fat' people in Auschwitz.

The worst way to lose weight is to eat less and go jogging – this doesn't work and makes you a moron. One: Eating less makes you hungry – eventually you'll cave-in. Two: Never jog. Never, ever, jog. Run or sprint but never jog. You want to get lean, right? Jogging won't help you. Jogging hardly uses any calories (might as well walk). If you're so heavy and out of shape that you can't run faster than a penguin, you shouldn't be reading Gang Fit *unless* you are determined that shit will end. Advice: Don't listen to any suggestions from a fat person. Ignore what they say, ignore what they do. Listening to a pod of fat people talking about diet and how to lose weight is like listening to poor people talking about how to make money – they're delusional, steer clear of them.

Generally,

1 Do some form of resistance training
2 Do high intensity exercise such as interval training
3 Eat no more than two meals a day
3 Reduce the carbohydrate content of your diet i.e., bread, pasta, rice, pizza, cakes, desserts, sweets. Eat as much meat, fish, eggs, non-starchy vegetables as you like.

More specifically,

LC HP IF – the way forward (diet)

LC (Low Carbohydrate)

HP (High Protein)

IF (Intermittent Fasting)

PA RT IT LA FT – the way forward (exercise)

[As well as helping you lose fat, this is your code for dynamic strength, fitness and robust health. It will enable you to achieve the physical targets in Gang Fit 2. Most of this they don't teach at school (another example of why school doesn't prepare you for real life, even though they say it does)]

PA (*Physical Activity*)

RT (*Resistance Training*)

IT (*Interval Training*)

LA (*Lactic Acid/Acidosis*)

FT (*Fast Twitch Muscle*)

At first glance this may seem like a lot; it isn't - it's the normal life of a wild carnivore. That's what you should be. It's only a lot of work for people who are used to wall-to-wall comfort.

LC - Reduce the carbohydrate content of your diet - bread, pasta, rice, pizza, cakes, desserts, sweets. Eat non-starchy vegetables

HP - Eat as much meat, fish, eggs, non-starchy vegetables as you like

IF - Eat two meals a day in a 6-8hr window. Breakfast and lunch or lunch and supper. Don't eat large meals late (within four hours of going to bed)

PA - Don't do all your physical activity in the gym. *Lazy people only go to the gym*, they do no other form of physical activity. This is unthinkable for someone who is Gang Fit, but many people do it. They never lose weight.

RT - Some form of resistance training 2-3 times a week is essential, it helps retain/build muscle whilst you are losing fat. Muscle is metabolic machinery; it keeps you lean.

IT - Interval training whether it is running, ergo, rowing, cycling is the dog's bollocks, do two sessions a week

LA - You need to reacquaint yourself with acidosis, a high heart rate and muscular effort, especially generated by the lower limbs. You do this as an interval training session. There is something about a lactic acid session which re-engineers the body.

FT - Engaging your fast-twitch muscle helps you build the dynamic strength and muscle of a wild beast

Don't fucking question how or why this shit makes you lean, it just does. If you exercise (and eat) like this it will be *impossible* for you to stay overweight.

Metabolic Test Kit

100m - ANAEROBIC

400m - ANAEROBIC, ACIDOSIS, aerobic

1 Mile - AEROBIC, ACIDOSIS, anaerobic

Easy 5k – AEROBIC

This example is running based, but you can use any physical activity you like in the way which utilizes these energy producing pathways – rowing, cycling, swimming, climbing; whatever. If you have developed and are retaining these three energy pathways you are virtually indestructible – you are as far from physical death as possible, plus your body is in the best shape to deal with environmental threats and diseases. Older people get weak, lose endurance, and can no longer tolerate acidosis (lactic acid). They literally lose the ability to generate energy. That's serious shit. Retain the ability to produce energy to stop getting old.

On top of this you may have your own test or metric which confirms you are in dynamic shape; the ability to sprint, do a backflip, jump up a 15ft wall, jump over a car, wrestle a tough opponent, deadlift three times your bodyweight, do one-hundred continuous squat jumps; whatever. Many people may think this is paranoid, but they are paranoid about keeping their jobs, having a monthly wage, and being a good slave. What *they* think is important means shit to you. Find out what is important you – develop it, retain it, test it.

Mash-Up Training

When he was young, Arnold Schwarzenegger, with his best friend, Franco Columbu, used to go to the lakeside in the woods near his village in Austria. They'd take meat for a barbecue, heavy metal (weights/barbells) and their current girlfriends. They would spend all day 'picnicking'; completing a hundred sets of barbell squats, swimming in the lake, eating meat and having sex. Ever seen a session like that in an exercise magazine? Arnie said this single session put half an inch of muscle on his legs. There was nothing his quads could do but explode. He couldn't walk for three days. This is raw, animal training. Testosterone, flesh, pleasure and pain. He didn't read that in a book. He was a beast – working-out, fighting, and taking steroids. All he wanted was growth; huge fucking slabs of muscle.

CHALLENGES:

1 Take your usual 5-rep max weight and do 10 reps. This sounds nonsensical, "a 5-rep max is the maximum I can do for 5 reps!". No, it isn't. It *definitely* isn't. You can double your rep count because you're only working hard, not super-hard. What you believe is your limit is nothing of the sort.

2 Lift 10-15% more than your maximum deadlift. To do this you will have to put yourself in a hyper-crazed state. The crazed state overwhelms fear. Fear is the *reason* you need to be in a crazed state, a state of rage. Your max is not your max, it's a pseudo-max. Note: Humans feel fear for a reason, usually for self-protection. The deadlift is the most fearsome lift, you could unzip your spine and end up competing at the Paralympics, throwing a shotput 75centimetres – that shit is definitely something to be fucking scared of. However, you regularly need to face your fears if you want to depart from normal society. The more you face your fears the stronger you become. Don't argue with this, it's true.

3 Take your 10-rep squat max and turn it into your 20-rep squat max. The demand this makes on your body is intense. You will feel like quitting after 15 reps, you'll feel light-headed - your legs will be burning and shaking from the acidosis and muscular fatigue. But keep going until you get through it.

4 Mash-up training (it 'mashes' you up) is the hardest when you do legs. It makes you want to cry. Try a leg only month – nothing except your lower body. Take five leg exercises and perform 5 sets of 20 reps for each exercise. *500 reps* in total. That's Arnie-level training. Just make sure you have an easy way to get home. Three days later, do the same. Do *only* this for a month, nothing else. Eat 50% more and get a load of sleep. Your legs will hate you. Maybe you'll die.

This sort of training celebrates of life by implementing a sort of physical death. The soreness you get from it screams at you that you exist. Life is about feelings; without feelings you are dead. Physical feelings are as important as psychological or emotional feelings. The Sun on your face, climbing a mountain, the taste of lemon, or the searing pain of acidosis and battered muscle fibres. Mash-up training confirms that the atomic nature of life involves utter destruction.

"You're Obsessed"

A person who works 40 hours a week tells a person who exercises 5 hours a week, "not to be obsessed". Can you believe that?! Shit for brains thinks that spending eight hours a day in an office is normal, but spending a fraction of that time exercising is abnormal.

This is why there is no point mixing with anyone who has 'shit for brains' – they're retarded.

"Obsession" as far as they see it, is *essential* for you – it's the launch pad, the fuel, and the rocket. It doesn't matter what is driving your obsession – money, hatred, anger, excitement or fear, it's all good. Keep going, keep being obsessed – that's how empires are built. Empires which provide food and work for the fuckers who call you obsessed.

100 Slaves

Every free person needs one-hundred slaves. Unless you live in the wild, you need someone to sweep the streets, empty the bins, build houses, clean toilets, and so on. Life is made better because people are willing (brainwashed) to be slaves. They are not *your* slaves, you don't own them, leave them alone. They are slaves to the system. A system which you should use for your own benefit. Some slaves think they are free, some are happy, some are miserable, some feel trapped but are too dim to realise they can do something about it – whatever, you need them.

Slavery isn't dead, far from it; it is more prevalent than ever. That's great for you. Honour the slave, but don't be one.

Budgerigar

Like most Sunday lunchtimes I was drinking at the pub with mates - one of them, Orlando, told us (after a few pints) about a study he'd been conducting on his pet budgerigar. That was a time when 'budgies' were very popular even though many ended up escaping through the front-room window (people liked budgies but it looks like budgies didn't particularly like humans). Anyway, just before going to bed Orlando would put a sheet over his budgie's cage, this signalled to his feathered pet that it was time for sleep. If his budgie had been noisy, squawking some shit, it would immediately go quiet - the sheet 'switched-off' the budgie. In the morning when the sheet was taken off, his budgie started chatting again, in the way the noisy fuckers do.

The experiment:

The sheet my mate used covered the entire cage, effectively blocking out the light - like drawing the curtains before going to bed. Over a number of weeks he slowly reduced the size of the sheet so that eventually it was only a piece of material the size of a beer mat. Orlando found out it wasn't the dark which switched off the budgie, it was the act of putting a sheet on the cage. The little critter was responding to an instruction. Maybe my mate could have trained it to go to sleep with a click of his fingers?

****

Over the next few weeks following budgie story I spent less and less time going to the pub. I stopped going on a Sunday lunchtime. I realised I was becoming a birdbrain, doing the same shit every week, following the same routine. This is what the young people my age were doing, or so I thought – going to the pub, getting hammered and acting like losers. I was no better than Orlando's budgie. My background had brainwashed me into doing what other people my age were doing; work, drink, sleep, work, drink, sleep – like a robot. I thought I was free – far from it. My life was as programmed as the budgie's.

If you have been taking note you'll know that Gang Fit has no problem with going to the pub, for fucks sake – but when you do what everyone else is doing (and when they are doing it) *just because they are doing it*, that's when your brain has stopped working.

****

After a few pints of beer conversations are generally meaningless, even if they seem deep or important at the time. *Budgie study story* was the reverse of this; it seemed meaningless to my friends, just a stupid story about my mate's peanut-brained bird, yet it was actually a neat observation about the nature of human conditioning.

Ok, the budgie didn't actually stop me being a loser by grabbing me in its claws and taking me from loser-land to winner-land; stuff like that doesn't happen in real life – you have to do it yourself.

GANG FIT META-CHALLENGE

Remember the 2-Point Plan? This is the simple goal of the Meta-Challenge.

- **Get rid of the shit in your life**
- **Add in what you want from life**

No matter what anyone else tells you, these are the most powerful two lines in your life. Unlearn what you were taught – replace it with these two lines.

This is a one-year challenge. After a year your old life will be unrecognisable. It is terrifying – most people won't do it. If you are doing jack shit at the moment you have nothing to lose – apart from possibly being made homeless. If you are financially secure but hate your life, you need to risk some of that security to make your life better. Gang Fit has never been 'feel good' bullshit. It guarantees you can change your life but it doesn't guarantee you won't starve to death in the process.

Leave your job – engage your brain. This is an essential part of the meta-challenge. If you can't (or won't) do this at some point during the year, stop reading now. This isn't for you. If you're not employed, all well and good - you have less holding you back.

Where you are now: **Attractor Landscape**

Read these sections and *act* on them:

1 Leave Your Job
2 Fit Work Around Your Life
3 Start Something
4 Get Fit, Get Strong

****

ATTRACTOR LANDSCAPE

The *Attractor Landscape* was a tool first created in the field of physics but has since been used to help an understanding of many other disciplines; genetics, neuroscience, robotics, political alliances and other stuff which people who think they're important talk about. It's also a good model for how to change a life of domestication, obesity, ill-health, mental prisons, depression and unhappiness, i.e., zombiefication. If you're young that shit shouldn't be much of a problem right now but it will be if you follow the usual advice.

It also shows why *everything* can change in an instant, either by your own volition or by a change in circumstances beyond your control.

People are stuck in their routines, environment and relationships. Some may be good and beneficial, ok - but others are negative. Eating junk food. Not looking after your health. Settling for a life of financial hardship. Living in an area you hate. Supporting Arsenal Football Club - and other lunacy. Despite 'efforts to change', people fall back into their usual routine. How does the attractor landscape help us understand this?

154

An Attractor Landscape

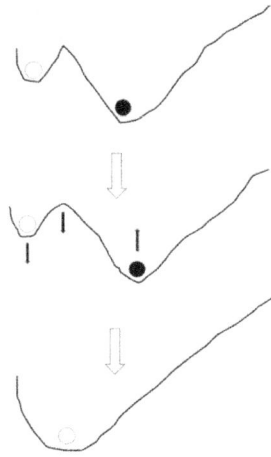

Source: Guru

You are the black ball. The valleys are the *basins of attraction*. The ball runs downhill to a basin of attraction and stays there - minor events or situational changes may move it but it settles back to stable (sort of) conditions. The depth of a valley is how much energy it takes to escape the attractor. An example could be that you hate your job, but the pay is good. The *width* of a valley is the range within which the attractor, attracts; you could say it's the amount of influences in your life that keep you where you are.

Top: A landscape with two attractors. A dominant attractor (black ball; the one you are in) and a latent attractor (the white ball) - where you would like to be. The latent attractor is better health, living somewhere nicer, having a six-pack; whatever.

Middle: Three dynamics change the attractor landscape. *Firstly*, the latent attractor gets stronger (it gets deeper) Maybe because your health is deteriorating. You can see the increased benefits of being in it. You are more dissatisfied with life. Something has happened which makes it more obtainable. You talk to people who are living it. *Secondly*, the dominant attractor gets weaker. You are more dissatisfied with life. You lose your job. Arsenal FC goes bankrupt. *Thirdly*, the 'hill' between the attractors gets smaller – it is easier to cross. You have saved money, so can take a risk. You get some sort of offer or opportunity in another city or country. A new gym has opened. You start a new relationship.

155

Bottom: The black ball has gone. The latent attractor has become dominant. You have escaped your old life.

The attractor basin you are in *necessarily* reinforces itself. It is self-referential and self-preserving. Its dynamics are the 'attractor' that means you do follow the same boring routine every day. Things around you want you to stay where you are. External and internal forces meaning you never change, never get fit, never leave shit relationships, never stand up to people who treat you like dirt, you stay timid and useless.

There was a study about a group of unconnected individuals who took part in an experiment where they had to live in a cave (something like that) for a month. Shut off from their usual influences and realities of life, on release, half of them decided to change their lives - even though they had no intention to do so before they went in. Just being outside of their basin of attraction for a while was enough to give them the impetus (kick up the arse) to change. The self- reinforcing dynamic of the attractor had been cut off. A different environment had given them a glimpse into new horizons and possibilities.

If something doesn't change, nothing will change.

If you don't change yourself or your environment, everything stays the same - you will continue in your basin of attraction, *unless* the environment or dynamics change (outside of your control) which forces you to change (divorce, redundancy, an accident, a stroke, a lottery win, meteor strike, shark attack). Even then, when there's an ecosystem change, many people choose to return to normal as soon as possible. Normal (the usual life) is what they know.

If you are stuck in a life you don't want, or want to avoid a life you don't want (look at the people around you) - stop pissing about like a loser:

- What are the *attractors* keeping you where you are?
- How *deep* are the valleys, or 'basins of attraction'? (deeper = harder to escape)
- How *wide* are the valleys? (wider = bigger range of attraction)
- Can you *move* the hills? (change the environment)

Again, your landscape can change in three ways:

1 By your own making

2 An external event (redundancy, divorce, childbirth, volcano eruption, winning the lottery, etc)

3 Slowly over time (positively or negatively)

The meta-challenge is the first one – a conscious attempt to change your landscape.

1 LEAVE YOUR JOB

Leaving your job is the most important thing you can do to change your life. There are different ways to approach it but it is the number one component of the meta-challenge. It's not optional, it's *mandatory*. If you are bargaining with yourself over this, you are not serious about wanting to change. You're just another bullshitter. You cannot hold on to your job and change your life. Develop and expand a side income whilst you are in it, but you have to leave at some stage. Don't irritate me.

Photo: Courtesy of Alessandro Riolo

Look at the above photo; the tall guy at the back. Someone told me about him.

"My granddad fished in the Newfoundland banks in his childhood, walked over a sleeping sperm whale as a teenager, harvested coral and sponges in his youth, raced the swordfishes as a young man, directed the mattanza of tunas as a man, and farmed in the salt pans in the old age. The picture was taken at Sfax, Tunisia, second half of the 40s. The guy on the left was my great uncle, his brother-in-law and life-long business

157

partner. They weren't employed a day in their lives. Sicilian fishermen were after shares of the bounty".

Many men would leave their jobs to live a life like this. Excitement, adrenaline, danger and wildness. No boss, just a band of brothers sharing the results of hard work, each willing to put their life at risk to save another. Pure fucking Gang Fit. Our ancestral heritage.

2 FIT WORK AROUND YOUR LIFE

Fit Work Around Your Life. Because this is so important, you are not taught it at school.

Years ago, before dinosaurs ruled the Earth, I had a dream of living on a desert island but with an internet connection. Living in Nature with access to the grid. Thanks to nerds and geeks, this has now become possible for millions for people. Anyone who wants it can get it.

Photo: Lucia Simeoni (*A Wood in Corsica*)

Part of fitting work around your life is that work is no longer work in the commute, trapped in an office, my life is shit, sense. It's entirely different. You don't hate work. It has a real purpose. It improves your life.
Whatever beliefs and visions you have in your head, that's what you need to go towards, don't be 'realistic' and compromise. Being realistic has created millions of boring lives. Be uncompromising. There are powerful forces that try to make you to fit in; this is why it's essential to be *actively* creating your life as you see it.

The problem is that millions find employment, then fit their beliefs to work and the working week – they become institutionalised. The beliefs they had when they were younger slowly dissolve until they become husks, non-people; robots. You can tell these people by the phrases they use; "have a good weekend!"; "Where are you going for your holiday?"; "What do you do for a living?". You know that shit isn't for you. No kid ever wanted to be like that.

Your *business plan* is to do only the things which maximise the odds of achieving the life you want. The most content people on the planet are doing just that. Only a zombie's preferred lifestyle is a full-time job. Business owner, self-employed, employed, freelance, creator - all that is irrelevant. The new economy and unlimited opportunity means the motivated individual can prosper.

Every time there's a commuter train strike 0.001% of the employed decide to leave the rat race. That's because they have hit the limit of what they can tolerate; some small event is enough to start a revolution. From now on you should only do things which are congruent with fitting work around the life you want. That's your revolution. If your life, health, job, relationships and environment are crap, tomorrow will be crap as sure as a bear shits in the wood. There are some parts of modern life which are good, take those but ruthlessly drop the things which are negative.

50 Weeks Vacation, 2 Weeks Work

Them: 50weeks work, 2 weeks vacation

You: 50weeks vacation, 2 weeks work

Whilst on a nice holiday, away from their usual life, how many people decide that 'things will change' when they get back (a new job, relationship, less commuting, losing weight). However, once they return they slip back into their normal routine and behaviour? They're pathetic. Modern life traps people into thinking what they do or feel on vacation is temporary while working their nuts off for a monthly wage is normal.

Organise a life where you don't *have* to get up for a wage, and you have no master who tells you what you can or can't do. Use the vast power and network of the grid for your own ends - the only point of the Grid. You control it, it doesn't control you. Whilst people are on holiday, you work, whilst they're working, you're on holiday – a parallel universe.

The Acute and the Chronic

Modern life is characterised by the transfer of the acute to the chronic. The acute things which make us stronger (or kill us) have given way to chronic work, chronic exercise, chronic food intake, chronic boredom, chronic medication, and the slow drip of chronic stress. The chronic leads to physical and psychological fragility. The desire to escape the feelings of entrapment derives from out hunter-gatherer nature. People need some sort of structure, but they don't need domestication. Some people are quite happy being domesticated, being half-human. You're not. The modern life of chronic routine, is no different to chronic eating – it makes us ill.

Chronic income is the only form of 'chronic' which is good for you, but you want to divorce it from chronic work. Chronic income with chronic work is slavery, chronic income with intermittent or hardly any fucking work is freedom. "But that's not possible for everyone!" Who cares? That's good. A free person needs people who work 9 to 5; and the reverse, the employed live off the backs of people who create stuff and start businesses.

Immensity-Ness

Be *immense* in 20% of your time, then you can relax or fuck about 80% of your time. Keep doing this and eventually you'll be able to fuck about for 99% of your time. As a friend said, "hard work, works...but you know what's better? Realising that a fraction of the effort gets you most of the results, and recognizing what fraction to focus on. Then you can use the remaining time to do whatever you want, without being beholden to anyone and without consequential risk". Clever guy.

This is how you escape the Rat Race.

3 START SOMETHING

There are only two types of income (regardless of source) chronic income (the amount can be 'guaranteed' or variable) or lump sums. If you have a huge lump sum it may not be necessary to have chronic income, although you would be advised to engineer an income from it as well.

Both are good; the lump sum carries you through lean times when there is no regular income; and a regular income feeds you whilst you are trying to make a lump sum. The lump sum you accumulate when you work will help you survive after you have left your job. A 'side hustle' (a bullshit term) can grow to generate enough income to allow you to leave employment – you have enough to pay the bills and eat

If you have don't have savings because you don't earn enough you have to 1/ get, obtain, borrow, enough money so you can survive for six months; 2/ or create a separate income whilst you are still employed; 3/ leave work anyway and hope you can generate enough ideas to create some money to keep the wolf from the door; 4/ a combination of these.

Unlike most advice, Gang Fit knows it is possible survive on credit cards, unsecured/secured loans, borrowing from friends, bank of mum and dad, and so on –

but it is risky. The downside is you run out of money, you alienate people, you can't repay your friends, parents or bank - your credit rating gets obliterated. There is also welfare, free money from the State. You shouldn't have any problem with claiming this *as long as it doesn't make you lazy*. The downside is that the state hassles you to get a job, and people think you're a scrounger – fuck that, most people like free money. If Universal Basic Income comes in, you can leave your job knowing you will not starve to death. Fuck anyone who tells you they pay tax so that lazy spongers like you can live off the state. If it's legal, do it. Gang Fit has mentioned this before, if free money makes you lazy, demotivating you from improving your life be very careful about accepting it. If it doesn't, take it. When you make money and start paying taxes you'll be paying back into the system (if that's how you care to view it. Gang Fit doesn't give a shit because life is unfair and there are no rules accept your progress).

Certainty - Uncertainty

Certainty: $250 per week every week. Uncertainty: $125 to $1500 per week; varies. Which one is better?

Uncertainty, risk, variability – apparently these are bad; you need security, safety, and knowing you can pay the bills. Ok, but there's a downside to extreme certainty: I was at an annual Christmas get-together I have with old friends from school. It's gradually become more depressing, they only talk about 'old times' – anyway, someone suggested we should meet up for a day out during summer. Here's what one of my mates said, "I'll have to look at my work schedule". I responded, "you know what you're going to be doing six months ahead?" He replied that he received a one-year work timetable at the start of every year. He could look up any day and see if he'd be working and what hours he'd be doing. What sort of bullshit is that? Might as well be dead. The spontaneity and randomness sucked out of life and replaced by certainty. Since then I haven't gone to any more get-togethers. These people have nothing for me. They look different (like shit). They talk different. They think different.

If you want to change your life; if you want an interesting life, you have to embrace uncertainty. Run towards it. The underbelly of uncertainty is opportunity, experience and feeling alive. A life without these is dead. Yes, it's good to know you can eat and pay the bills; beyond that certainty has no merit if it is coupled with a boring shit life. That's the certainty and security of a cemetery.

The ironic thing is as your empire grows, "certainty" becomes irrelevant and positive variability takes over. Yes, you may lose money, or not make sales, or a project won't succeed, but that won't be forever. Expose yourself to the upside (volatility, serendipity, surprises) and limit the *really* stupid shit.

161

I understand there is a warmth to security, but it can make you torpid, you are smothered by it. Knowing *exactly* where your life will be in one year is a curse if it means you become fossilised. The meta-challenge is a journey, it doesn't know the destination.

Safe to Fail Experiments

If you scatter five hundred seeds on different soils, in different conditions, and forty-five germinate, you haven't used computation, analysis, luck, targeting, research or probability to get results. You don't care about the seeds which didn't germinate. The seeds cost fractions of a penny. The idea of 'safe to fail experiments' (or, *small bets*) is to pursue new opportunities without spending too much money (or time) on any one opportunity. You may have a mega-project you are working on which may pay back big sometime later. However, if it doesn't, you will have wasted lots of time and maybe too much money. Note: One of the good things about having no money (or access to money) is that you don't waste it on speculative ideas, business start-ups and risky shit. Come up with ideas, information, helpful aids, etc., *then automate them* – take out the admin and grunt work as much as possible. A traditionally self-employed individual (plumber/personal trainer/builder) needs to put in the hours; they charge for their time, ok; but they can only increase their income by doing more hours or increasing how much they charge per hour – which has a limit. A well-paid solicitor or doctor can charge a lot for their time but there is this still an income ceiling, and it comes with long hours. But if you have a business or an automated system which allows people to buy your product, service, information, idea, course; whatever - you can earn money whilst you're asleep, on holiday, at a party, or in a brothel. New technology and the internet enables you to automate almost anything. Automating your ideas means you can earn money with minimum hours (the immediate, medium, or long-term objective, depending on your motivation) – not earning money with maximum hours.

Crisis Management

People think that crisis management is only necessary when there is a crisis. Nonsense. Your entire life is a 'crisis' in that if you do nothing it turns to shit, if you do a mega-

wrong thing it can turn to shit, if you allow others to control you it turns to shit. Life is a long crisis. This doesn't mean that life is bad; life is good, don't be ungrateful – only that if you don't take *some sort of action*, life will be a slow downward spiral into crap. Potential untapped; no use to anyone.

The US Marines have the motto, 'improvise, adapt, overcome'. Don't get stuck in your usual mode if it's not working. This means you might have to turn what you normally do upside down to stay ahead, grow, or even to stay alive. This is the same idea as the OODA Loop (*observe–orient–decide–act)*, developed by US Air Force colonel John

Boyd in the mid-20th century, to prepare soldiers for combat operations. In environments (your new life) which may be volatile, uncertain, complex and ambiguous, the prize goes to the individual who can react to changing circumstances quickly and efficiently. Think back to the 'Street Olympian' essay in Gang Fit (Pt 1) – a real example of a teenager who out-ran a 800metre Olympian by utilising the variability of his environment…*'the street kid was a product of his terrain; agile and clever like a wild-animal. He utilised his environment, jumping over walls, zipping up stairs, getting through gaps, under things and over things - taking advantage of his surroundings.'*

There is more; in his book, *An Introduction to Cybernetics* (1956), Ross Ashby introduced his *'Law of Requisite Variety'*. Known as the 1st Law of Cybernetics. Ashby was primarily interested in homeostasis (in living systems) - the way in which complex systems, operating in changing environments, succeed in maintaining equilibrium within tightly defined limits. Important: His law proposed that if a system is to be able to deal successfully with the diversity of challenges that its environment produces, then *it needs to have a range of responses which is (at least) as varied as the problems thrown up by the environment.*

What this means is that you have to be adaptable, develop skills, develop your innate talents and most important of all *act on them*. Nothing will happen if you *only think about doing things;* action beats thinking every fucking time. Stop writing lists, stop researching, stop fucking about – **start something!**

4 GET FIT, GET STRONG

There is no true freedom without health, it's just not possible + being dynamically strong and fit makes you feel like a boss. Even if you are working hard to create freedom in your life, never forget about your health. Poor health ruins everything.

Base physical targets (from Gang Fit 2):

Deadlift: One-rep max of 2 x body weight (general strength)

Chin-ups: 20 (usable upper body strength)

100m sprint: Under 13 seconds (speed)

One mile: Under 6 minutes (endurance)

Body-fat: 10-12% - a six-pack is just visible (health)

How?

Resistance training – weights, circuits, and calisthenics

Intervals (HIIT) – short to long (anaerobic/lactic/aerobic)

Daily low-level activity

Occasional 'mega' challenges

Loading:

45% Resistance training

45% Interval training (short to long, anaerobic/aerobic')

1-2% Mega-challenges

~ 8% Random – mini & micro-challenges.

You don't have to be autistic about this and copy it word for word – use your brain. There are sessions you can use in Parts 1, 2 & 3.

Note: There may be other physical targets which are meaningful to you – you may be a dancer or train for a sport, whatever. That's good. Eat well. Keep active. Keep strong. Stay healthy.

The Gang Fit Meta-Challenge - You Have One Year

Balcony of Dead Flowers

A teenager who'd left home (because of 'trouble') moved to a flat in a different part of the city. A nice flat, with a communal garden, in a nice area. The flat had a small balcony. For the first few years the balcony was covered with plants and herbs growing from terra cotta and ceramic pots. A bird feeder on one side, and on the other, a solar-powered night light for sitting out on warm summer nights. Moths, bees, butterflies and birds would visit. Everything in life was good.

As our teenager headed towards her mid-twenties, things in her life began to turn sour; a failing relationship, a dissatisfying job, a feeling that something important was missing. On the outside she was her same self, but on the inside she was depressed. You wouldn't have known there was anything wrong with her. There was only one outward sign that something was wrong - the flowers on her balcony began to die. She no longer watered or cared for them. Nature's small creatures no longer visited. She no longer sat outside on a summer evening.

This lasted a few years, but one day she met a new person, a person who was right for her. She left her job and started an enterprise based on what she loved doing. Over time she felt happier, in fact she felt *very* happy, and guess what? Yes, Einstein – her balcony sprang back to life. Nature returned. An occasional Owl hooted "*hello!*" on a summer night.

****

What has this got to do with you? Gang Fit doesn't give a shit about religion or 'supreme beings' but when you gaze at beauty you are viewing the face of God. When you turn your back on beauty you are turning your back on all that is good in life. Beauty is the key to life, it can be found amidst the most terrible destruction and hurt. If your life is shit you need to create something beautiful – even if it's only one thing. Having something beautiful in your life protects you from all the shit around you. It's the world's most powerful shield.

Your life is a garden, you want it to flourish. It may be redesigned every now and then, that's ok – quite normal. Many elderly people who have died leave a well-tended and loved garden behind, their life's work, only for that garden to fall into disrepair – an indicator that you if you don't tend to your life other forces take over. What about their partner? Here's the thing, when a person who has been in a 50-year relationship dies, their partner dies withing six months, they have no reason to live, they give up; unless their children take over, the garden dies with them. Sad.

If your life has turned into a 'balcony of dead flowers', for whatever reason – fucked-up dreams, a lost relationship, a dead parent, or just the feeling of despair and hopelessness, you have to keep going, regrow your flowers and make them beautiful – you tend to them, they will give back to you.

****

Gang Fit is street, it doesn't give a shit what people think; it hates zombies, it detests full-time employment, and it says that violence is sometimes necessary to protect your independence and sovereignty – *but its main message is that you need to create beauty in your life.*

Thank you for reading Gang Fit

Printed in Great Britain
by Amazon